+HD30.28 .P325 1984

Y0-DLT-010

```
HD      Paul, Samuel, 1930-
30.28
P325    Strategic
1984    management of
        development
        programmes
```

DATE DUE

JUL 26 1997		
SEP 04 1997		
	JUL 18 1998	
	JUN 29 1998	
	JUN 29 1998	
AUG 05 1999		
NOV 08 1999		

due 7/5/05

Demco No. 62-0549

Strategic management of development programmes
Guidelines for action

Samuel Paul

Prepared with the financial support
of the UNDP Interregional Programme

Management Development Series No. 19
International Labour Office   Geneva

Copyright © International Labour Organisation 1983

Publications of the International Labour Office enjoy copyright under Protocol 2 of the Universal Copyright Convention. Nevertheless, short excerpts from them may be reproduced without authorisation, on condition that the source is indicated. For rights of reproduction or translation, application should be made to the Publications Branch (Rights and Permissions), International Labour Office, CH-1211 Geneva 22, Switzerland. The International Labour Office welcomes such applications.

ISBN 92-2-103252-3

First published 1983
Fourth impression 1990

The designations employed in ILO publications, which are in conformity with United Nations practice, and the presentation of material therein do not imply the expression of any opinion whatsoever on the part of the International Labour Office concerning the legal status of any country, area or territory or of its authorities, or concerning the delimitation of its frontiers.
The responsibility for opinions expressed in signed articles, studies and other contributions rests solely with their authors, and publication does not constitute an endorsement by the International Labour Office of the opinions expressed in them.
Reference to names of firms and commercial products and processes does not imply their endorsement by the International Labour Office, and any failure to mention a particular firm, commercial product or process is not a sign of disapproval.

ILO publications can be obtained through major booksellers or ILO local offices in many countries, or direct from ILO Publications, International Labour Office, CH-1211 Geneva 22, Switzerland. A catalogue or list of new publications will be sent free of charge from the above address.

CONTENTS

Introduction 1

Chapter 1 Development programmes: concept and scope .. 5

   1.1 Promise and performance 6

   1.2 Nature and scope of development programmes .. 9

   1.3 Programme phases 17

Chapter 2 Pre-conditions of performance in the
          public context 21

   2.1 Three constraints 21

   2.2 Pre-conditions of performance 24

   2.3 Guidelines for programme designers and
       managers 29

Chapter 3 Strategic management: the basic factors 33

   3.1 What is strategic management? 34

   3.2 The concept of congruence 38

3.3	Top management's role	39
3.4	Points to remember	42

Chapter 4 Reading the environment 43

4.1	The role of environmental analysis	43
4.2	Scope, diversity and uncertainty	49
4.3	Search for information	52
4.4	Guidelines for environmental analysis	55

Chapter 5 Formulating the programme strategy 57

5.1	The basic influences on strategy	57
5.2	The service-beneficiary-sequence (SBS) strategy	60
5.3	The demand-supply-resource (DSR) strategy	66
5.4	Some guidelines for strategy formulation	71

Chapter 6 Structure: the key dimensions 75

6.1	Structural forms	76
6.2	Degree of decentralisation	84
6.3	Organisational autonomy	86
6.4	Some guidelines for structural choices	89

Chapter 7 Process interventions 93

| 7.1 | Governmental processes | 93 |
| 7.2 | The participation process | 95 |

7.3	Human resource development processes	99
7.4	The monitoring and control process	101
7.5	The motivation process	104
7.6	Some guidelines for programme managers	106

Chapter 8   <u>Orchestration of congruence</u> 109

8.1	The meaning of congruence	110
8.2	Congruent combinations: some illustrations	111

Chapter 9   <u>Putting strategic management into action</u> ... 117

9.1	Preparing new development programmes	117
9.2	Applying strategic management to ongoing programmes	121
9.3	Taking action	125

Appendix 1   <u>Further reading</u> 127

Appendix 2   <u>Glossary of selected strategic management terms</u> 137

INTRODUCTION

A wide variety of development programmes operate in the Third World today. Governments and international donor agencies have spent considerable amounts of money on them and are concerned about the viability and performance of many of them. Increasingly, it is being said that their planning and implementation leave much to be desired. Even those with the right technologies and enough funds seem to perform poorly. It is not surprising, therefore, that "management" has been identified as a neglected factor. The realisation that technology, capital and management are complementary is an important step forward in understanding development programmes.

Unfortunately, little knowledge exists on how to organise and manage development programmes. Traditionally, the focus has been on the technology and economics of programmes, not on their management. The bureaucrats and managers of programmes were left to improvise and muddle through. Invariably, they ended up adopting the systems, practices and administrative processes common in government. No doubt, specialised techniques and tools were sometimes borrowed to improve decision making. Thus budgetary reform or new systems for recruitment were sometimes introduced. But no over-all framework exists for thinking about and planning for the management of development programmes.

This book is a modest attempt towards filling this important gap. It presents an approach to the "strategic management" of development programmes. The concept of strategic management developed here draws upon the current

1

management literature and related disciplines, and derives support from a recent international study of several successful development programmes.[1] The meaning, scope and significance of the strategic management of development programmes are discussed in detail in the following chapters; they are based on an analysis of the characteristics that the successful programmes shared.

In chapter 3, strategic management is defined as the inter-related set of top management interventions which create the framework within which operational decisions and actions are taken to accomplish the goals of a development programme. To create this framework, programme managers must pay special attention to four main influences on a programme's performance. These are the programme's environment, strategy, structure and processes.[2] The essence of strategic management is to create a "fit" among these so that the programme gains from their internal consistency or "congruence". Strategic management refers to the process by which top managers identify and influence these factors, and continually create a fit among them. If the operating decisions and actions are to improve the performance of development programmes, the starting point must be the practice of strategic management.

This book is written for programme leaders and managers first of all. In a development programme, it is the leader who must initiate the practice of strategic management. Only he or she can create the institutional framework within which other members of the organisation can operate effectively. The ideas and guidelines in this book are, therefore, addressed to the programme leader and the top management team.

Management development institutions constitute another

---

[1] For details of the study, see S. Paul: Managing development programmes: Lessons of success (Boulder, Colorado, Westview Press, 1982).

[2] These terms are discussed in detail in chapters 3 to 7. A summary of strategic management is presented in chapter 3. References for further study are appended at the end of the text.

very important audience of this book. Many of them have identified project and programme management as a priority area of the interventions in the forthcoming years. They are keen to increase their impact on development programmes by helping to analyse problems faced by managers, design and apply more effective management and control systems, define and introduce appropriate criteria of programme performance, and provide various types of practically oriented training in programme and project management. The book should provide some guidance both for the practical analysis of problems faced by programme management and for the design of management training programmes which address these problems.

The approach to strategic management presented here will also interest ministers and other policy makers, administrative heads of ministries and donors who initiate and oversee development programmes. These people are responsible for providing the framework within which programmes are designed and operated. When they do this poorly, the performance of programmes suffers. Programme managers undoubtedly need their support and understanding in order to practise strategic management. Only when policy makers and donors understand the implications of strategic management can they create the pre-conditions to make it work. In this sense, the strategic management approach is equally relevant to the political and administrative leaders and technocrats in government and donors who play entrepreneurial and supervisory roles in development programmes.

Our focus is strategic management; we do not explore the problems of operational management that development programmes face, even though these are important, and programme managers do spend significant time on them. A discussion of operational or short-term problems would have made this book too long, and information about operational management is available elsewhere. In fact, most of the consulting and training programmes today are largely concerned with this class of management problem, e.g. performance evaluation, budgeting, pricing, etc. What is lacking is the larger framework within which these problems can be more readily identified, analysed and solved. Strategic management should, therefore, assist programme leaders to solve operational problems better.

Finally, a caveat is in order. Strategic management is not a panacea for all the ills of development programmes. When the basic policies of a country are in disarray, its manpower shortages severe, and its financial resources scarce, it will not be able to get its development programmes off the ground. If good leaders cannot be found, programmes will suffer. When people are not motivated, their response to programmes is bound to be limited. Countries differ in the degree to which their peoples are performance-oriented. This problem of achievement motivation is characteristic of many developing societies. It is a constraint which should be considered in assessing the environment of any programme. To put these matters in perspective, the pre-conditions for strategic management are discussed in chapter 2. But the pre-conditions alone do not guarantee good performance. Strategic management is vital even when all the pre-conditions are met.

The book has nine chapters. The nature and scope of development programmes are explained in chapter 1. Chapter 2 examines the pre-conditions of performance in the public context, in which most development programmes are designed and carried out. The concept of strategic management, its components, and their interrelationships are discussed in chapters 3 through 8. The end of each chapter contains questions and guidelines to facilitate a review of the concepts discussed and to help the manager apply them to his or her specific situation. In training programmes, teachers and trainers may wish to use these questions with case studies or experiences of programmes. The concluding chapter 9 offers practical suggestions for policy makers and programme managers on how to put strategic management into action in the particular context of a new or an ongoing development programme.

DEVELOPMENT PROGRAMMES: CONCEPT AND SCOPE

1

It is nearly three decades since macro-economic planning became fashionable as a tool of development in the poorer countries of the world. Macro planning, also known as development planning, was expected to give a sense of direction to national economies and provide a basis for allocating scarce resources among the priorities for development identified in national plans. Irrespective of their ideologies, many developing countries, which became politically independent in the 1950s and 1960s, were soon attracted towards systems of national economic planning. The scope and sophistication of planning, of course, varied considerably from country to country. Thus India formulated and publicised a series of "five-year plans". Nigeria adopted six-year plans, whereas many other Asian and African countries have had three and four-year plans.

Macro planning entails varying degrees of public intervention in economic and social activities. Development plans consist not only of patterns of resource allocation and long-term national budgets, but also certain strategies for developing different economic sectors. The pace and type of development of agriculture, industry, education and other social services are spelt out in the plan documents. Since the private sector is limited in its capacity to raise the resources and is often regarded as an inappropriate instrument to implement the proposed changes, the State decides to actively intervene and manage many new development activities. This is true not only of infrastructure development such as roads, ports, communication and power, but also of certain categories of industry and critical support systems required for agricultural and rural development. Thus irrigation projects, agricultural extension services and common facilities for small industry development, to cite just a few, are usually promoted under public auspices. Such public interventions are usually termed "development programmes".[1] A macro plan consists of several development programmes, depending on the public interventions being envisaged during the plan period. It has been estimated that in many less developed countries (LDCs), nearly 50 per cent of the annual budgets of governments are spent on development programmes.[2] The development plans and programmes of LDCs, therefore, consume a significant share of their resources.

1.1 Promise and performance

Though most developing countries have allocated significant resources to development programmes over the past two decades, performance has not matched expectations. In some countries and in some sectors, results have been impressive. But over-all, the performance of development programmes is by no means encouraging. The impact of development programmes on rural areas, where most people in the developing world live, has been dismal. Almost 20 years ago, Waterson observed:[3]

> With many factors accounting for the inability of most countries to achieve targets in their plans, a question arises whether one factor - more than any

---

[1] Sometimes they are also called "public programmes". We shall, however, use the term "development programme" in this book.

[2] Economists use the term "development expenditure" to differentiate this category from the normal maintenance expenditure of governments.

[3] A. Waterson: Development planning: Lessons of experience (Baltimore, Maryland, Johns Hopkins University Press, 1965), pp. 332-333. See also U. Lele: The design of rural development (Baltimore, Maryland, Johns Hopkins University Press, 1975) and Public service delivery systems for the rural poor (Bangkok, United Nations ESCAP, 1980).

other – is responsible for this inability. Until very recently, it was thought that the key element in the planning process was the formulation of an economically consistent plan. While the importance of a well-prepared plan based on clearly defined development objectives is indisputable, it was not generally realised that a consistent plan does not ensure implementation any more than an inconsistent one. When the plans they had prepared were not implemented, planners trained as economists assumed, and still assume in some circles, that the failure to achieve targets was mainly attributable to errors in computing and allocating resources or to errors in basic data.

The widening gap between promise and performance has opened the eyes of planners and policy makers to the limitations of macro planning. Planning is a useful aid for choosing development goals and allocating resources. But planning alone does not ensure performance. In many countries, planners have refined their methodologies and introduced new planning models. But there is little correlation between the sophistication of planning and national performance. This realisation has led some planners and international agencies to focus on how to formulate better programmes and projects. A consistent macro plan is still practically useless unless the projects and programmes which constitute it are well conceived and selected.[1]

By far the greatest number of failures to carry out public sector projects and programmes at reasonable cost in reasonable periods of time are traceable to inadequate project selection and preparation. Few less developed countries are fully aware of the necessity for selecting soundly conceived projects with potentially high yields, defining their scope with clarity, estimating their national currency and foreign exchange requirements with a sufficient degree of accuracy, and laying down realistic schedules for their execution; fewer yet have the administrative capacity and the potential will to cope with these needs and, especially, to carry out plan projects and

---

[1] A. Waterson, op.cit., pp. 320-321.

programmes in accordance with carefully developed programmes of action.

In the late 1960s, many countries began to recognise the importance of designing projects competently and choosing them carefully. Project appraisal tools became popular in many planning agencies. National and international organisations disseminated new ideas on project appraisal and cost-benefit analysis through their "manuals".[1] Attention thus shifted from macro to micro planning. Leading financial institutions, such as the World Bank, now conduct careful project appraisals before they lend money to LDCs for specific schemes. Country officials are trained to used the new methodologies and a new kit of tools has been added to the development planners' armoury.

Analysing the costs and benefits of industrial and conventional infrastructure projects is relatively easy. Technologies are known, demand can be estimated, and monetary calculations are not terribly difficult to make. But, with the growth of development programmes in social sectors such as education, health and nutrition, many assumptions of the new methodology have been called into question. Technologies had to be evolved or adapted. Estimates of demand or public response have generally turned out to be extremely misleading. Projects that were considered viable when formulated and appraised turned out to be low performers when implemented. Even industrial and infrastructure projects, though carefully prepared and evaluated, have actually performed poorly.

Thus, a new class of problem has been identified as responsible for poor performance. It now seems that inadequate attention has been paid to the implementation of projects and programmes. Decision making is tardy and organisation arrangements for managing the projects are vague. Even when projects were physically completed, too little attention was paid to getting them to perform well and to maintain the facilities. Many observers have called this set of issues "management problems" and have argued

---

[1] For example, UNIDO: Guidelines for project evaluation (New York, United Nations, 1972) and I.M.D. Little and J. Mirrlees: Manual of industrial project analysis in developing countries (Paris, OECD, 1969).

that the widening gap between project and programme plans and their performance is largely due to management failures. Unfortunately, planners too often view implementation and management as issues outside their purview. The dichotomy between planning and implementation prevailing today in many countries reflects an inadequate appreciation of the interaction between the two. Planners are reluctant to recognise feedback on implementation problems as an input to the planning process. Further refinement of planning tools and models cannot possibly make up for the deficiencies in implementation and management.

This brief review reveals a gradual evolution in our understanding of developmental processes and performance. The concern about management of development programmes can be traced to the dissatisfaction with the performance of development plans and programmes. This does not imply a rejection of planning. Macro planning, micro planning and public management are complementary, not subsitutes for each other. This book focuses on the management of programme. What is special about development programmes and makes them difficult to manage?

1.2 Nature and scope of development programmes

Development plans typically consist of numberous programmes organised and managed by public agencies. Even countries without such macro plans have many programmes managed by public agencies. Thus development programmes are found in all developing countries, including those who do no macro planning. Agriculture, industry, health, education and housing are important sectors where development programmes have been undertaken. The rice production programmes in the Philippines, the family planning programme in Indonesia, the rural electrification programme in India, the adult education (literacy) programme in Tanzania, etc., are sectoral programmes. Programmes have also been organised for the development of infrastructure such as roads, communication and other public utilities. In some countries, infrastructure and common facilities for small industry development may be provided through an industrial estates programme. Many countries commonly organise such programmes through agencies created by ministries or departments.

Sometimes, development programmes are organised for specific regions or areas in a country. For example, irrigation programmes are feasible in defined areas for physical and geographic reasons. Some countries have programmes to develop backward regions with special authorities or agencies to plan and integrate the different inputs and facilities needed to promote development there. Venezuela's development programme for the country's Guyana region is well-known. India and Brazil similarly have special programmes for their backward regions. Sometimes, sectoral programmes which are nominally national in scope may in fact be confined to limited areas. Agricultural crops may be grown only in certain regions. Thus, the smallholder tea development programme of Kenya operates only in 12 out of nearly 50 districts because tea cannot be grown everywhere.

The third category of programmes are multisectoral integrated programmes. Some sectoral programmes for single commodities or services integrate different inputs and activities to promote the commodity or service under the same programme. Thus the Kenyan programme for tea not only provides extension services, but integrates it with credit, leaf collection, processing and marketing. On the other hand, integration may occur across sectors as in integrated rural development programmes. Though the scope of such programmes varies widely, most are based on the concept that income-generating activities and social services which enhance the quality of life should be provided simultaneously in order to facilitate sustained rural development. This programme design calls for the integration of agricultural development with the provision of health and education, and related infrastructural facilities. According to a recent UN report:

> The concept of integrated rural development, and thus the resulting programme configuration, is likely to be defined differently in different settings and in accordance with the definers' frames of reference. Various definitions have been examined at international meetings, and new ones have come out of such meetings. However, there appears to be no overwhelming evidence that fundamental changes in definitions have been made. The current definitions of IRDP, like the old, refer to the interface and mutual reinforcement between social and economic development at both

national and sub-national levels, to the consequent need for comprehensive approaches to rural development, to the importance of popular participation and local decision-making and to the multi-faceted character and breadth of the development process. Current definitions, again like the old, refer to integrated rural development in both substantive and procedural terms and subsume combinations of purposes, strategies and outcomes in the definition itself. However, the current definitions more explicitly identify the poor in the rural areas as the principal clients, and more directly aim programmes at such specific goals as employment, increased agricultural production, augmented income and equitable distribution thereof and greater access by the rural poor to public services.[1]

Integrated rural development programmes are now common in the developing world. In the Philippines, a new integrated rural development programme is being carried out under the supervision of a cabinet sub-committee. Colombia has an Integrated Rural Development Programme. Mexico's PIDER is a national programme to develop rural infrastructure. Many integrated rural development projects operate in limited geographical areas.[2]

Some programmes which started as single sector projects later evolved into multi-sectoral programmes. This was the case with the Cameroon Land Settlement Scheme which expanded into a broad integrated socio-economic development programme. In many countries, all these different types of programmes operate simultaneously. Thus in Kenya, the smallholder tea development programme operates alongside the Special Rural Development Programme. Many programmes emerge as adaptations to local conditions, problems and needs. The "commodity" as against the "area" approach, or "national" as against "regional" scope do not

---

[1] <u>Public administration institutions and practices in integrated rural development programmes</u> (New York, United Nations, 1980), p.6.

[2] For a detailed discussion of such programmes see ibid. Also see <u>Rural development: Sector policy paper</u> (Washington, DC, World Bank, 1975).

necessarily represent right or wrong choices, but rather options, appropriate in certain conditions, inappropriate in others.

Our threefold classification of development programmes can help us understand the complexity and scope of public interventions. <u>Sectoral</u> programmes generally aim to develop a single commodity or service nationally. <u>Regional</u> programmes also develop sectoral services, but in sub-national (regional) areas. <u>Inter-sectoral (integrated)</u> programmes focus on several sectors and call for a careful integration of diverse sectoral inputs. National integrated programmes exist but are rare. Sectoral and regional programmes are most common, with integrated inter-sectoral programmes gaining in popularity. This classification, however, helps little in judging the superiority or viability of a programme. Many other things must be considered, as we shall explain in subsequent chapters.

Irrespective of classification, all development programmes are "instruments" of public policy and "intermediaries" between the beneficiaries at the grassroots and national or regional governments. Traditionally, governments implemented policy directly through ministries and departments without the "intermediation" of special agencies or institutions. Thus tax collection, maintenance of law and order, etc., have always been managed departmentally without creating separate organisational entities. Development tasks, however, necessitate the creation of new instruments that can better acquire and process complex, specialised and diverse inputs to meet the needs of specific segments of the population. This is the rationale of development programmes.

Development programmes are usually conceived at the national level and operate through sub-programmes designed to cover different geographic regions such as states or different functions and groups of services. A rice development programme might have sub-programmes for extension, irrigation, credit, seeds and fertilisers, each broken down regionally. The sub-programmes in turn might be a series of discrete, interrelated or sequential projects integrated into a relatively permanent delivery system. Programme implementation is expected to occur through its location and service specific components which interface with clients or beneficiaries where they live or work. Thus, for example, agricultural or small industry development programmes may deliver their services through units set up near the farmers or entrepreneurs throughout the region or country.

The terms "projects" and "programmes" are often used interchangeably. Project orientation often dominates because aid agencies tend to design and promote pilot projects or limited-area projects. However, major institutions such as the World Bank have been involved in broader, ongoing activities. The development and management of national or regional programmes to replicate pilot project results are usually the responsibility of the governments. There are, of course, some projects which are of a continuing nature, e.g., irrigation projects. Donor agencies tend to be involved in such projects for a short or medium term. Donors' time perspectives, therefore, tend to be shorter than those of national governments, which have long term responsibilities to manage such projects. Donors' relatively limited involvement in larger programmes partially accounts for the comparative neglect of programme management. Pilot projects and limited-area projects are to national programmes what research and development (R&D) projects are to large corporations. The products the corporations sell often result from R&D projects, but the corporations' problems of managing commercial production and marketing of such products are distinctly different from, and often more complex than, the problems of managing their R&D projects. Similarly, the management problems of large development programmes are different from those of the pilot projects which supply the "products" to be replicated by programmes. The problems of large programmes also differ from those of the smaller, simpler time-bound projects.

By neglecting to study the larger, national programmes, we have ignored an important class of public management problems.[1] This gap must be filled, because the

---

[1] Interestingly enough, scholars located in developing countries or who have opportunities to be in the field have paid greater attention to the problems of such national programmes. Of course, if countries have not gone beyond the stage of pilot projects, opportunities for such involvement cannot possibly exist.

replication of project results occurs almost solely through the medium of larger programmes. The ultimate test of the success of pilot projects is the extent to which they are replicated or adapted nationally. The author of a study of selected pilot projects in developing countries once concluded that they were successful because their technical findings were promising. Further investigations, however, revealed that none of the countries extended, adapted or replicated any of these projects. One cannot seriously attribute success to projects that have failed this basic test of replicability.

Studies of development programmes and projects reveal a strong <u>sectoral orientation</u>. Since most donor agencies and LDC governments are organised sectorally, projects and programmes are dominated by sectoral technologies and contexts. Public management problems then appear unique to each sector and cross-sectoral comparison and learning is resisted. For example, few health programme managers know much about agricultural programmes and what each could learn from the other. Researchers follow similar paths. Developments in the theory and practice of public management have consequently suffered.

Sectoral differences do require different management practices.[1] Programmes which provide direct and immediate economic gains should be managed differently from those which do not. Entrepreneurs respond eagerly to industrial development programmes likely to generate profits, whereas illiterate villagers may not want to participate in a preventive health programme. Programme management practices must allow for such differences, but inter-sectoral comparison is necessary to identify which successful practices can be transferred and where distinctly different practices are called for.

---

[1] L. Stifel et al.: <u>Education and training for the public sector in developing countries</u> (New York, Rockefeller Foundation, 1977), p.7. US scholars who have worked on public programme implementation have, on the whole, avoided the sectoral bias. Comparisons across sectors and departments have been a part of their general approach. The problem has been more serious for scholars working on LDC programmes, possibly because of their long-term sectoral involvements.

To understand better the nature and scope of development programmes, four distinctive features are outlined below:

Policy sanction

Normally, a specific legislative enactment precedes the creation of a public programme. Thus an authoritative decision of the government stands behind every development programme. The concept of policy sanction is applicable even in countries without development plans. US public programmes, for example, have appropriate legislative approval behind them. In countries with national development plans, an executive decision suffices, since the national plan containing the programmes has legislative approval. Presidential decrees, acts of parliament, etc., reflect formal, authoritative government decisions.

Development focus

In contrast to regulatory programmes whose developmental impact might be indirect, development programmes are expected to generate economic and social outcomes (measurable and immeasurable) consistent with national development goals such as income growth and distribution, and improved quality of life. Their tasks are such that the discipline of the market mechanism is rarely an adequate framework for planning and controlling their operations. Development programmes, therefore, fall between purely regulatory programmes at one end of the spectrum, and commercially oriented public enterprises at the other.

Organisational identity

A development programme is an entity with its own organisational structure, budget and personnel. Even a programme under the administrative control of a ministry or a government department has its own organisational structure, assignments of tasks and responsibilities and reporting relationships. Development programmes can thus be distinguished from temporary systems and short-lived experimental projects. They are usually set up as authorities, boards, councils and other bodies with their own organisational identity. They may be fully or partly financed from government sources. Some may be self-financing agencies.

Replication

A programme's mission tends to be the replication or adaptation of a "developmental product" or "service" over the entire country, or some of its constituent regions to benefit specified client groups. The developmental service need not be a physical commodity; it may be a system designed to deliver a product or service in a specified geographical area and determined by the techno-economics of the sector or sectors and the existing geographic and organisational conditions. Thus in a health programme, the service is not the set of individual health services (which are, of course, of direct concern to the beneficiaries), but the system designed to assemble and deliver them at the village, sub-district, or district level. Similarly, it may be misleading to define the output of a dairy development programme as the "supply of milk"; its service might well be a system to integrate services to produce, process and market milk to benefit specified client groups. It is this system which a pilot project tries to test, and a which national programme tries to replicate and adapt over large areas.[1]

The "service" underlying a development programme is either developed indigenously, or designed abroad and borrowed or adapted from foreign experience. Borrowing or designing models from abroad is extremely common among industrial programmes. Agricultural, rural development and social service programme designs are less easy to import. In fact, such models may not even exist. The concept of the service must then be developed indigenously. Whatever the approach, there is likely to be an identifiable service that a programme attempts to replicate. Again, the nature and scope of the service might well change with experience. The needs of the clients may change, necessitating changes in the service. Serious problems arise in large development programmes when services are specified inappropriately or the service or output is poorly understood.

---

[1] The design of the individual services or end products is an important technical rather than management problem. Projects and programmes have to generate design, production and delivery systems which enable beneficiaries to receive the intended services, consistent with available resources and norms of efficiency.

1.3 Programme phases

Policy sanction, development focus, organisational identity and replication characterise all development programmes whether sectoral, regional or inter-sectoral. Pilot projects, experimental interventions and "crisis" programmes rarely possess all these four features.[1] However, development programmes which have all these features are not necessarily permanent. Some have permanent missions, others are phased out over time. We need, therefore, to examine their "life cycles".

Life cycles of development programmes can be divided into phases which sometimes overlap. The pilot phase is the initial period when a "product" or service is being designed or adapted. This may or may not precede the formal launching of a national programme. The Mexican rural education programme organised by CONAFE started with a pilot phase when experimental work was done in a hundred community schools. The Philippine Rice Programme benefited from a pilot project involving 10,000 hectares. Pilot projects did not precede the Indonesian Family Planning Programme, but were undertaken concurrently with the programme. Many large programmes suffer either because pilot projects were never thought of or useful feedback from such experiments was lacking.

The replication or adaptation phase begins when the programme is extended from the pilot area to other areas. This phase offers the maximum challenge to the strategic and operational management of the programme. The growth in the size and complexity of the programme due to spatial expansion creates tough management problems which cannot be studied in the pilot phase. A pilot project confined to a few villages can be supervised personally by the project manager. He manages with simple systems and informal face-to-face relationships. The problems of a complex organisational structure (e.g., motivation and control of personnel, and decentralisation) rarely arise in the pilot

---

[1] We are here referring to pilot projects which have not been consciously planned to lead to larger programmes. Crisis programmes are short-term emergency programmes to deal with catastrophies like floods, droughts, famines, etc.

project. These occur only when the project is extended or replicated on a larger scale.

Once a programme has completed its replication phase, its <u>maturity phase</u> starts. Depending on the type of service, the maturity phase takes one or three forms: (1) it may continue indefinitely as long as the service is needed (e.g., the generation and supply of electricity, health services, etc.); (2) it may be terminated if the service is no longer required or the client groups or private agents can take over (e.g., agricultural extension and input services, family planning, etc.); (3) the programme may be diversified, taking on new tasks, but carrying on the original service as part of its broadened mandate. For example, population or health programmes sometimes diversify to provide nutrition services without giving up the original services.

Management problems are most severe during the replication phase because formal systems must replace informal relationships in the course of "scaling up" from the pilot phase, and during the maturity phase if the programme becomes diversified.

Figures 1.1 through 1.4 illustrate the phases of a programme's life cycle and the different options it may choose at maturity. The horizontal axis represents time in years and the vertical axis represents the geographical coverage. In the pilot phase, coverage is usually quite limited. The time taken to complete the pilot phase is often small compared to the programme's life cycle. During replication, geographical coverage increases. Maturity signifies stability, both geographically and in service delivery.

Figure 1.1 depicts the life cycle and phases of a development programme that takes on permanent services. Figure 1.2 represents a programme which, having fulfilled its mission, gradually winds down and terminates its service during its maturity phase. In figure 1.3, the programme divests itself of one service upon reaching maturity and develops another, repeating the cycle.

"Sequential diversification" is depicted in figure 1.4; service I continues permanently and service II is then added, starting from its own pilot phase. The prog-

Figure 1 Life cycle and phases of a development programme

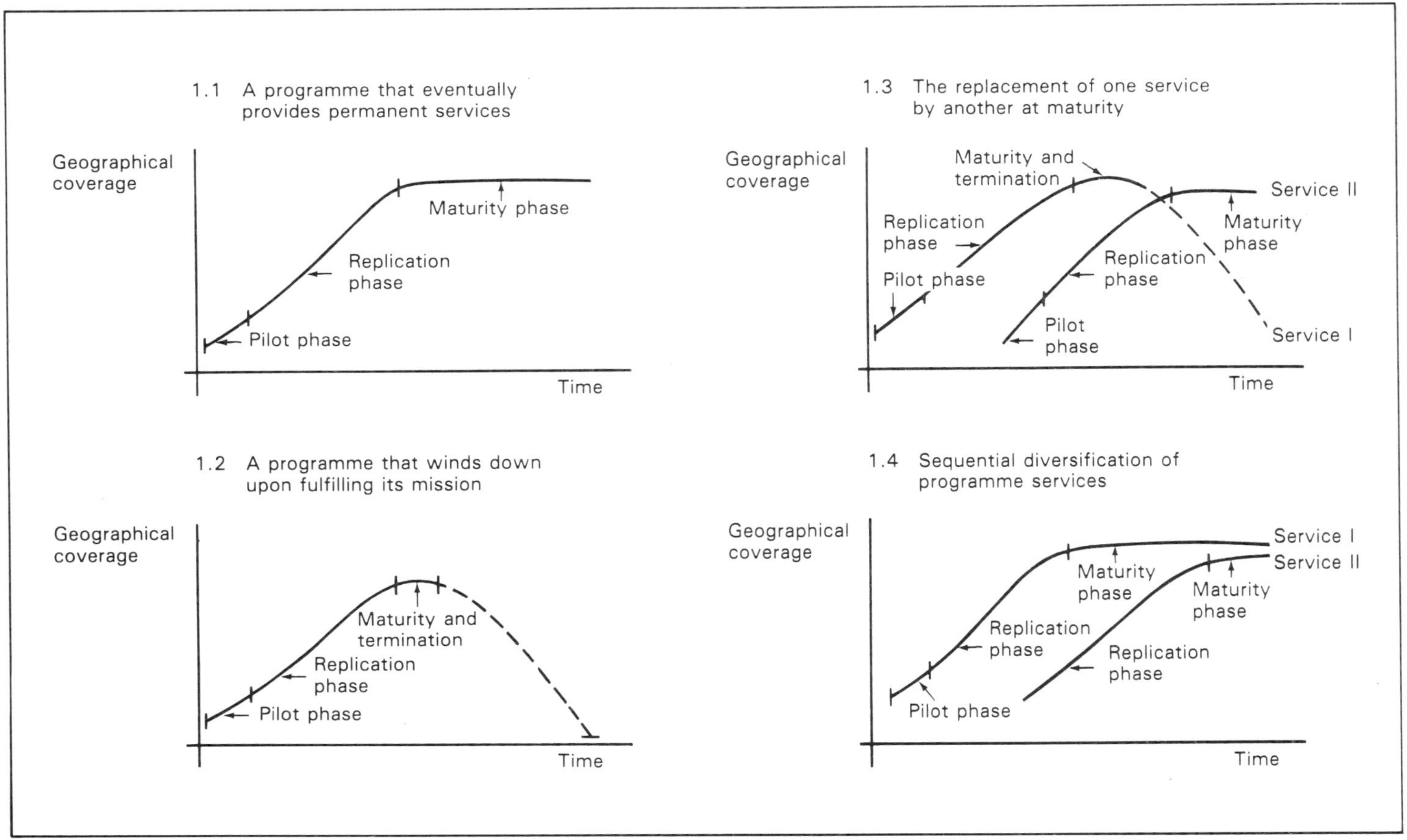
1.1 A programme that eventually provides permanent services
Geographical coverage
Maturity phase
Replication phase
Pilot phase
Time
1.2 A programme that winds down upon fulfilling its mission
Geographical coverage
Maturity and termination
Replication phase
Pilot phase
Time
1.3 The replacement of one service by another at maturity
Geographical coverage
Maturity and termination
Replication phase
Pilot phase
Service II
Maturity phase
Replication phase
Pilot phase
Service I
Time
1.4 Sequential diversification of programme services
Geographical coverage
Service I
Service II
Maturity phase
Maturity phase
Replication phase
Replication phase
Pilot phase
Time

ramme thus diversifies sequentially and offers both services on a continuing basis.

All these alternatives can be found in different countries, even though not all programmes have formal pilot phases. In some programmes, experimental or pilot projects may be concurrently undertaken when the programme is initiated. This was true of the Indonesian Population Programme. The country already had some experience with family planning when the programme was launched. Many programmes have come to grief because the pilot phase was skipped and programme strategies did not take into account the features of the national or regional environments. Some programmes compensate for the lack of a pilot phase by limiting their geographical spread initially and expanding their scope carefully through a learning process.

In summary, awareness of management problems of development programmes is growing as experience accumulates on the limitations of macro and micro planning. Development programmes have emerged as important instruments of public policies articulated in development plans, but are common even in countries which do not practise macro planning. Programmes must be distinguished from pilot projects and other temporary programmes which lack organic links with the more durable public interventions. Four common characteristics of development programmes are policy sanction, development focus, organisational identity and replication. Development programmes need not be permanent. It is useful to delineate three phases in their life cycle, namely the pilot, replication and maturity phases. A programme may continue to operate permanently when it offers a service in continuing demand or diversifies to provide new services which meet the long-term needs of beneficiaries.

THE PRE-CONDITIONS OF PERFORMANCE AND THE PUBLIC CONTEXT

2

Important differences exist between public and private management which make the public manager's task difficult. Coping with these constraints is part of the role of those who manage development programmes.

2.1 Three constraints

First, there are constraints on the choice of <u>goals</u>. The broad objectives to be achieved by a development programme are generally laid down by policy makers. A private enterprise, on the other hand, is largely free to choose its goals. A development programme may be given diverse or multiple goals, some of which may be conflicting. The outputs of a programme are often difficult to measure. A rural development programme, for example, may be expected to increase agricultural production, improve the conditions of the poorest people, and provide health and educational services to them. All these goals may have to be pursued simultaneously even if some of them conflict with each other. Private enterprises are seldom loaded with such a diversity of goals and expectations. The limited flexibility available to the public manager to choose programme goals is thus a constraint.

Second, those who manage development programmes usually have fewer <u>means</u> to choose from than those who manage private enterprises. This is because governments often prescribe the systems and processes of decision making in organisations which use public funds. In private management, means are more easily adapted to goals. Organisational processes and practices are more flexible. Results come first, means second. In public management, on the other hand, means are treated on a par with goals. The constraints on means often hold back goal attainment. The rigid norms prescribed for the purchase of goods and services, budgetary sanctions, and performance evaluation may be such that operational decisions consistent with efficient goal attainment may be discouraged. Thus public managers seldom get the instruments necessary to achieve programme goals.

Third, the orchestration of goals and means is often constrained. Goals and plans must be modified to match changing situations. The means to achieve goals must be adapted. But adaptation is difficult when goal setting and policy making are isolated from the process of implementation. Policy making and implementation can be separated successfully only if policy makers have enough information about implementation and the environment is stable so that midcourse corrections are unnecessary. Neither assumption is valid for most development programmes. Policy makers are seldom fully informed about the course of implementation nor can they anticipate all future problems. The external environment does change over time, necessitating frequent adaptations of policy and implementation decisions.

The public sector customarily assigns different sets of actors to the policy making and implementation roles. The goals and design of a development programme are usually specified by top government policy makers, including political leaders. Another set of officials, minimally involved in policy and planning, usually implement and manage the programmes. Political appointments at top government levels strengthen this cleavage. The people who establish goals and tasks thus commonly fail to understand implementation problems and those who implement often fail to understand the goals. Planning agencies, external donor agencies and high level staff groups in ministries design the policies and leave implementation to lower level civil servants, newly recruited managers or technical experts. Design changes usually require the approval of pol- icy makers.

Sharp cleavages between policy and implementation are rare in the private sector. There, managers at different levels are encouraged to generate policy-design ideas and interact actively with corporate planners before formal decisions on policies and designs are made. Chief executives play crucial integrating roles. Those who are called upon to implement or manage new projects or plans may well have been active participants in the initial formulation, and are given adequate powers to adapt to changing conditions.

It could be argued that the state has a greater control over its environment than the private sector does and that the task of goal-means orchestration is therefore easier for government agencies. But in practice, a public agency's ability to achieve such orchestration is limited for several reasons. The __large size__ of government with its centralised decision making processes and multiple programmes restrict manoeuvrability. The relatively weaker emphasis on __accountability__ for results reduces the pressure for achieving orchestration. The __diverse political pressures__ on programmes and the consequent compromises public managers make also weakens orchestration.

The three constraints on goals, means and goal-means orchestration operate in varying degrees in all development programmes. Many cases could be cited to show how programme performance was hurt as a result of delayed responses to the need to adapt to changing conditions. Slow approval from higher authorities in government and slow concurrence of donor agencies weaken orchestration at the programme level. This problem is by no means unique to LDCs. Studies of public programmes in the USA in urban development, employment generation and education[1] provide evidence of similar constraints in developed countries too.

If a programme is to succeed, government should choose goals consistent with the means available or adapt the means to fit the goals, and create organisational structures and processes which facilitate the orchestration of the two. The failure of most governments to fulfil these conditions makes the task of public management more

---

[1] See J. Pressman and A. Wildavsky: __Implementation__ (Berkeley, University of California Press, 1971); M. Derthick: __New towns in town__ (Washington, DC, The Urban Institute, 1972); W. Williams and R. Elmore (eds.): __Social programme implementation__ (New York, Academic Press, 1976).

complex and onerous. The private manager has more control over these matters than his public counterpart. Those who manage development programmes thus start with a handicap. Exhortations to public managers to practice what is best in private management ignore the significance of the relative difference between the two environments.

2.2 Pre-conditions of performance

Performance of development programmes is influenced by more than quality of management. While management interventions are an important determinant of performance, many observers have noted the critical role of political commitment and support, resource availability and the quality of programme leadership in facilitating successful outcomes. Programmes which lack these cannot perform satisfactorily even if managers are competent. A useful way of characterising their role is as follows: political commitment, resources and leadership are enabling conditions. Their presence facilitates the contribution that management interventions can make to improved performance. Let us examine the three pre-conditions.

<u>Political commitment and support</u>

All public decisions are, in the final analysis, political. A decision to allocate increased funds to rural development or set up industrial estates to support small-scale industry reflects some political commitment to these policies and programmes. The degree of political commitment and support to different programmes varies. The stronger the support and political consensus behind a programme, the greater the likelihood that programme managers will work in a favourable environment. Thus when a president, prime minister, cabinet or other key groups which wield political power are seriously committed to a programme, many external and internal obstacles which normally constrain good performance can be removed or weakened. Similarly, where top political support is feeble or nominal, programme managers find it difficult to mobilise the needed resources and achieve the intended impact. This applies even to policies and programmes included in national development plans. No effective action on policy decisions and programmes can be taken even when they are part of a plan. Often, the problem can be traced to a lack of political commitment. Some pilot projects and more durable programmes sponsored by donor agencies also experience the same fate. New projects may be initiated by an LDC government goaded on by a donor. When the latter withdraws, the projects fall apart or are not extended. Analysis often shows that there was no strong political commitment to these projects from the outset.

How a programme is set up tells us much about the political commitment behind it. Figure 2 depicts two alternative routes which political leaders often take in establishing development programmes. Top political leadership should be broadly interpreted to cover the top bureaucrats in a country who advise political leaders and whose views therefore influence final decisions in these matters. Route A is typical where a political policy decision is made to launch a development programme. The need for a public intervention is established, but detailed strategies are not worked out. Instead, a search is started for a suitable leader to plan and manage the programme. When the key leader is identified, a public agency is formally created or adapted with a broad mandate to formulate a strategy and mount the programme. It is the programme leader or manager who then draws up the detailed strategy and recommends plans for implementation including the organisational structure. Route A clearly reflects a high degree of trust in the programme leader by the political leadership and the latter's willingness to share "power" with him in the programme's planning and implementation.

Route B also starts with a top policy decision. The sequence of decisions or actions from then on, however, is quite different from that of Route A. The policy decision is followed by the specification of programme goals and strategy. A programme agency is established and its organisational structure is designed. The key programme leader or manager is then appointed. His responsibility is to implement the programme. Here, the political decision is followed by a sequence of actions which do not involve the programme manager. He steps in only as an implementor. The strategic choices have already been taken by the top political-bureaucratic personalities. This is a classic illustration of the policy-implementation dichotomy. It also reflects a relatively low level of political commitment and support. The "power" allocated to the programme leader is limited and there is little appreciation of the need for interaction between policy and implementation by the programme leader.

Figure 2 Establishing a development programme: sequence of interventions

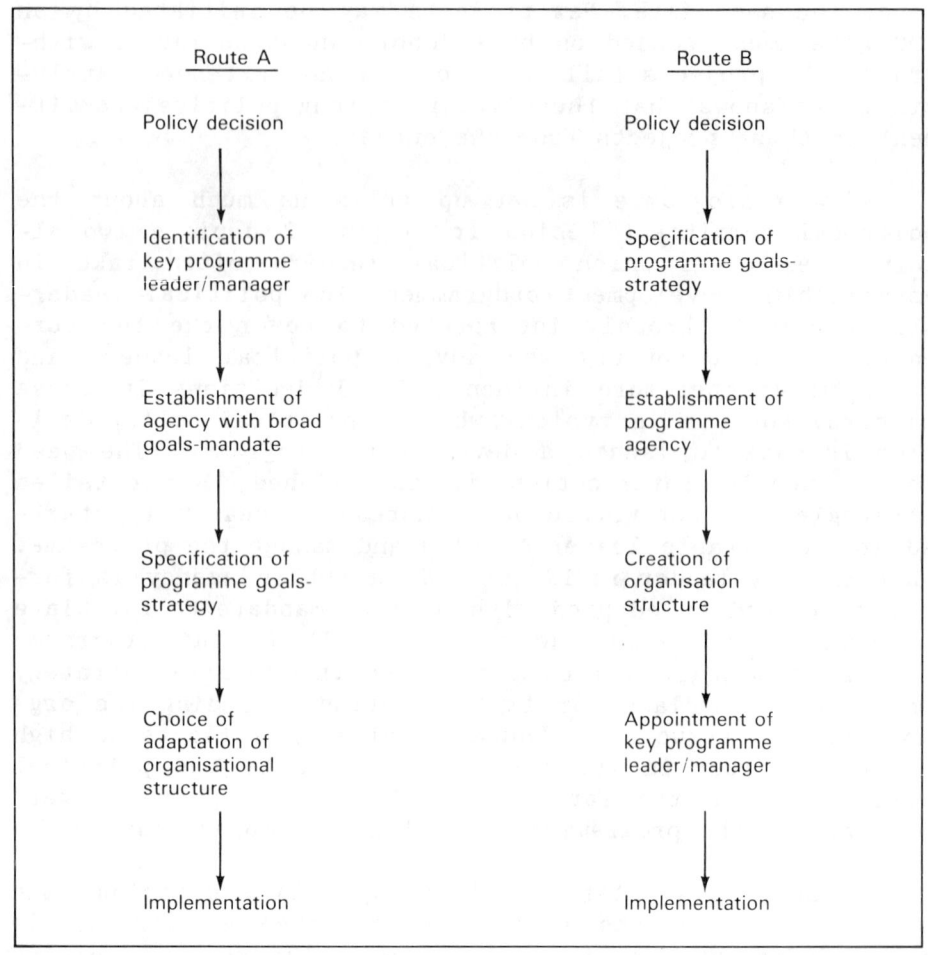

Routes A and B are stylised versions of two extreme approaches to the sequence of decisions which flow from policies to programmes and finally to implementation. In reality, the sequences are likely to fall somewhere between the two extremes. They are, however, useful in understanding the enabling role that top level political commitment and support plays in the management of development programmes.

Route A may be taken also when the political–bureaucratic leadership finds it difficult to operationalise highly complex projects and programmes (technologically) along route B. In such cases, a programme manager may have considerable latitude and room for initiative. Scientist-managers in some countries who organised atomic energy programmes and other technically complex projects benefited from this, though in these cases political commitment was not deliberately planned. In effect, the consequences for the programmes and their managers were not significantly different.

Resource availability

No programme or project can achieve results without adequate resources, both financial and human. A programme with strong political support usually gets adequate resources. However, poor countries, in spite of political commitment, usually lack adequate funds. Often, funds may not be made available on time. Severe skilled manpower constraints may render implementation extremely difficult. Unlike private commercial enterprises, some development programmes may not be able to raise their own resources, although, in fact, good public managers may also find innovative answers to resource problems.

In both private and public programmes and projects, the issue of resources should be separated from that of management. In the private sector, when a new venture is launched, the generation of resources is seen as a priority task. The board of directors which approves and supports the new project, also allocates adequate funds and manpower to get it going. The same approach holds good for development programmes. Resources thus are a pre-condition for programmes and projects. When this condition is not fulfilled, the ability of programme leaders to perform their tasks will be severely constrained. Good management cannot be a substitute for financial resources and trained manpower. Rather, these are the essential inputs on which good managers build. Resources are a pre-condition because resource availability by itself (like political support) cannot make a development programme perform. Some analysts differentiate between physical and technological resources, and financial and human resources. But financial and human resources can be used to acquire physical and technological resources. Thus technology and some of the basic institutional infrastructure required (e.g., budgeting, personnel systems, etc.) can be bought or adapted and new facilities or physical assets can be created. Many programmes have resources in abundance, yet fail to deliver the goods.

Leadership

Development programmes, especially large new ones, need good leadership for two reasons: (a) planning and initiation of new programmes require entrepreneurial thinking. The person picked to lead a programme, therefore, should have entrepreneurial characteristics such as strategic vision, creativity, initiative and willingness to take risks and try out new solutions; (b) he or she should be capable of mediating between the political leaders and the environment of the programme on the one hand, and the programme's administration on the other.[1] The leader's commitment to the programme, his or her ability to build teams and develop and motivate people, and skills in building linkages should be distinguished from the management interventions which we shall discuss in the rest of the book. The leader's ability to motivate his or her staff and beneficiaries will, of course, be influenced by their attitudes and values in terms of achievement orientation and team work. Countries differ in their achievement characteristics, a factor which programme leaders must be sensitive to, and take into account in their practice of strategic management.

The choice of the programme leader is directly related to the degree of political support and commitment attracted by a programme. When top political leadership is strongly committed to a development programme, the search for a suitable leader will usually also be seriously undertaken. A person thus identified is more likely to enjoy the trust of the political leadership than one selected routinely without active support from the top. Since the quality of programme leadership is critically important to programme performance, it should be treated as a precondition for programme success. Top political support is usually necessary for a programme to get enough appropriate resources; thus appropriate programme leadership cannot be over-emphasised.

Political commitment, resources and leadership alone do not guarantee success. Nor can well-planned management

---

[1] For a discussion of the mediating role, see H. Mintzberg: "Patterns of strategy formulation", in Management Science, May 1978, pp. 938-940.

Figure 3 Probability of programme success

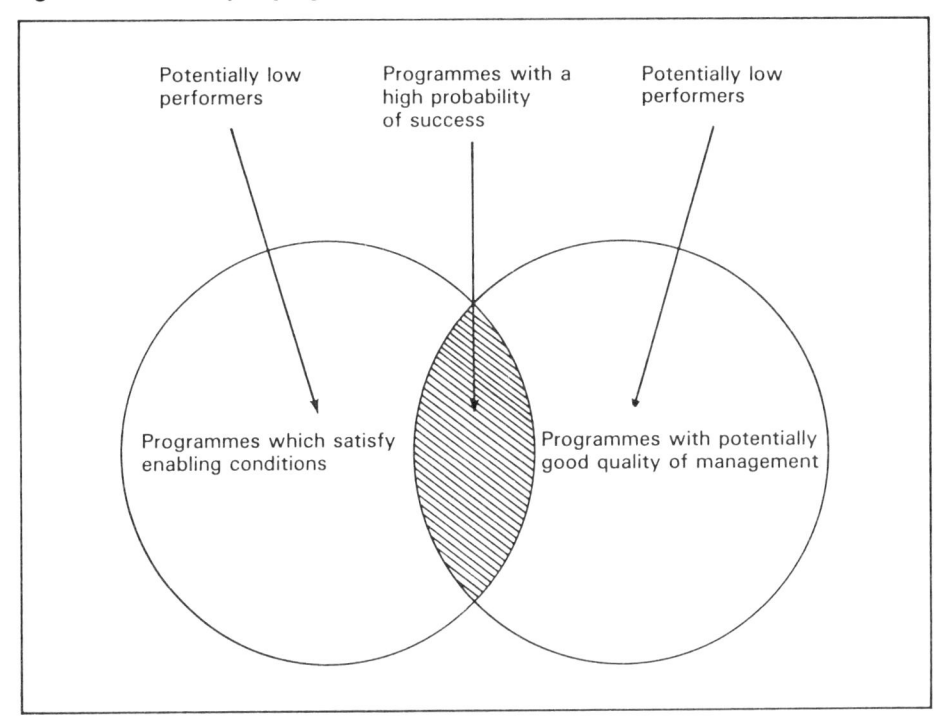

- Potentially low performers → Programmes which satisfy enabling conditions
- Programmes with a high probability of success → (intersection)
- Potentially low performers → Programmes with potentially good quality of management

interventions alone guarantee good performance. As figure 3 illustrates, only those programmes which have both good management and proper enabling conditions are likely to succeed. Programmes on the left-hand side will perform poorly because they lack pre-conditions. It is only at the intersection of these two sets that both conditions (satisfying pre-conditions as well as good management) are met. Only those programmes located where the two circles overlap meet both requirements and therefore have the potential for success. In designing programmes, it is important to ensure that these conditions are satisfied while simultaneously taking steps to strengthen programme management.

2.3 Guidelines for programme designers and managers

Those of you who design or manage new development programmes, or are called upon to restructure or adapt on-going programmes cannot directly control the pre-conditions discussed above. Nor can you do much about the constraints operating on programmes in general. You can, however, often influence them in your favour. The following guidelines and questions can help designers and managers do this:

Political commitment

1. How strong and stable is the political consensus behind the policy decision leading to the proposed programme?

2. Are the key actors in government (political and bureaucratic) concerned with the policy decision solidly behind the programme?

3. Has the Government spelled out in detail the goals and strategies of the programme or given a rather broad mandate?

4. Has the Government assigned an agency to be responsible for the programme and specified its structure?

5. Did the Government identify the person to head the programme prior to the setting up of the agency and specification of its goals?

6. Is there mutual trust between political and bureaucratic leaders and the programme head?

Resources

1. Is the Government likely to allocate adequate resources to the proposed programme?

2. Are the sources of funds for the programme fairly stable and reliable?

3. Is the top political commitment strong enough to ensure adequate resources to the programme in the future?

4. Are human resources (trained manpower, etc.) likely to be readily available to the programme?

5. Will the physical and technological facilities needed by the programme be available?

Leadership

1. Did the search for the programme leader emphasise entrepreneurial qualities?

2. Has the chosen leader been involved (is he likely to be involved) in the specification of programme goals, strategies and the structure of his programme agency?

3. Is he likely to be a pro-active leader or one who will merely be an implementor?

4. Is he capable of building teams, and developing and motivating people?

5. Does he show evidence of a strong commitment to the programme?

6. Is he inclined to provide continued leadership, given his terms of appointment, and the conditions and conventions in the public environment?

Definitive answers to these questions will be difficult to obtain when a development programme is being initiated. No one is likely to have enough information to come to conclusions on all these pre-conditions. On the other hand, the questions can help you assess the potential impact of the "pre-conditions" on programme performance.

STRATEGIC MANAGEMENT: THE BASIC FACTORS

3

It was argued in chapter 2 that development programmes perform well only when the pre-conditions of political commitment, resources and leadership are satisfied and competent programme management is practised. In this chapter, we probe the second part of this proposition. That good management crucially determines programme success will hardly be disputed by anyone. The problem is to define the focus and content of management. After all, managers and administrators in any development programme, or for that matter in any organisation, make many decisions and actions. If decision making is efficient, and actions and choices are based on competent analysis, and their implementation is effective, then the quality of management is high. But what makes this happen? Are some key management interventions critical to programme performance?

The answer appears to be that a set of key management interventions exists. Evidence from successful development programmes shows that critical interventions by top management decisively influence outcomes and provide a framework within which operational decisions and actions can be taken by others in the organisation.[1] An understanding of these interventions can help programme managers improve their performance and make operational decisions more purposeful and efficient. We shall call this set of top

---

[1] See S. Paul: Managing development programmes: Lessons of success (Boulder, Colorado, Westview Press, 1982) for an analysis of some outstanding examples.

management interventions "strategic management". When day to day management or operations of a programme are not informed or guided by proper strategic management, performance suffers.

3.1 What is strategic management?

There are diverse views on the critical dimensions of management in a development programme. Some argue that "good management control" ensures performance. Others emphasise the importance of "community participation".[1] Another group highlights political and bureaucratic bargaining processes as the major determinant of outcomes.[2] This diversity of views comes partly from the different types of development programmes which have been examined by different authors. For a rural education programme, whose outcome depends on the interaction between children and teachers, and adaptation to the local needs of communities, participation at the grass roots is important. An infrastructural programme to build and maintain roads, on the other hand, needs standard systems and good management planning and control. For regulatory programmes which require close collaboration among several public agencies (e.g. industrial development and licensing), political and bureaucratic bargaining may be crucial. Thus the dominant problems of different types of programmes lead observers to emphasise some management interventions and to exclude others. The proponents of different views have neither understood nor articulated the fact that their prescriptions emerge from an analysis of only a few programmes. We all generalise without fully realising how key interventions will differ with the environment and the nature of different programmes.

Strategic management therefore must consider four key

---

[1] See D. Korten: "Community organisation and rural development: A learning process approach", in Public Administration Review, Oct. 1980.

[2] J. Pressman and A. Wildavsky: Implementation (Berkeley, University of California Press, 1971); M.S. Grindle (ed.): Politics and policy implementation in the Third World (Princeton, New Jersey, Princeton University Press, 1980).

influences which together determine the performance of a development programme. These are:

(1) the external environment of the programme,

(2) the programme strategy,

(3) its organisational structure, and

(4) its organisational processes.

The performance of a programme is influenced not only by each of these factors, but also by how they interact, i.e. by the degree to which they are consistent with and reinforce one another. So top managers should try to influence each factor and also their interactions.

In any development programme, there are many factors at work, and a manager can easily get lost in a maze of details. The secret of strategic management lies in identifying the key factors. Successful agricultural development programmes, for example, emphasise evolving a package of inputs (seeds, fertilisers, water, practices, etc.) most conducive to increased productivity, price incentives to farmers to encourage them to adopt the new package, and creating a network of agencies to effectively plan and implement this strategy. These are dimensions which only top management can envisage and influence. They constitute a manageable set, and do not lead managers to lose sight of the forest for the trees. Perceptive leaders almost instinctively identify the critical factors relevant to their programmes and organisations. But in complex situations, commonsense alone may not suffice. An understanding of the key factors and ways of relating them to one's own setting can be of considerable assistance.

This may sound abstract and academic to the hard-headed practitioner. Let us therefore look at this framework and its components more closely. First, we shall define the key factors.

Environment

The environment includes the forces outside a programme which create opportunities for, as well as constraints on, its growth. The environment of industrial enterprises includes their consumers and their incomes and other relevant factors. The environment of an agricultural development programme includes the farming population, their levels of technology, water and soil conditions and climate. The environment of most development programmes includes prevailing political conditions, beneficiaries and the local institutional and bureaucratic set-up. These factors change at different rates, and from place to place. Top managers must not only be familiar with them, but also appraise the environment in order to identify opportunities for the programme's growth while minimising the impact of any emerging constraints. Favourable environments improve a programme's potential for survival and expansion. Unfavourable ones provide programme managers with difficult conditions and obstacles.

Strategy

Strategy is the set of long-term choices the programme leaders make in terms of goals, services, policies and action plans. Successful strategies must meet both the broad programme objectives set by government and by the environment. For example, a governmental programme to promote small-scale industries throughout the country must have goals and services consistent with the literacy and background of potential entrepreneurs, the potential demand for various goods and gaps in the infrastructure. Strategies that meet the government's objectives and match the environment are more likely to succeed than those that do not.

Organisational structure

The organisational structure of a programme refers to the durable arrangement within a programme agency to perform the tasks defined by its strategy. These include the distribution of authority and responsibility, the reporting relationships and the mechanisms for integrating its functions. Some strategies and environments require decentralised structures, others require centralised ones. When diverse services are offered, divisions based on the type of service may be appropriate. When the programme operates in far flung regions, a structure based on regions may be justified. Structures therefore are not fixed or permanent. Existing structures often limit the choice of strategies. Rigidities in government structures often limit the ability of conventional government departments to engage in commercial operations. Hence the practice of setting up government corporations when such needs arise. No single structure is good for all strategies and environments. Many development programmes fail because they are unable to adapt their structures rapidly to evolving strategies and changing environments.

Organisational processes

Organisational processes are the instruments for influencing the behaviour of employees and beneficiaries of a programme. If the staff of an organisation are to accomplish common goals, managers need the means to motivate and influence their performance. Participative methods used to set goals, allocate resources and implement the programme are one set of organisational processes. The monitoring methods for evaluating and controlling performance are another. Such processes and systems are commonly found in industrial enterprises. They are equally relevant in public programmes. Processes for human resource development (selection of staff, training, etc.) are another set of instruments. Too few programme managers seem to realise that these are not fixed processes and that to be effective, they must be adapted to particular strategies and structures. Thus the motivation processes for a family planning programme may have to be quite different from that used in a commercial crop development programme. The right mix of processes can improve performance; an inappropriate mix will be counterproductive. Proper organisational processes are sources of power and influence in the hands of top management when they are tailored to the strategy and structure of the organisation.

In the following chapters, we shall elaborate on each of these factors and explain how programme managers can analyse and influence each of them. For the present, let us summarise three important features.

(1) There are four factors, environment, strategy, structure and processes which influence programme performance.

(2) They are not independent. They interact. Environment certainly influences all others, but it can sometimes be influenced itself by management's strategy.

Figure 4 The basic components of strategic management

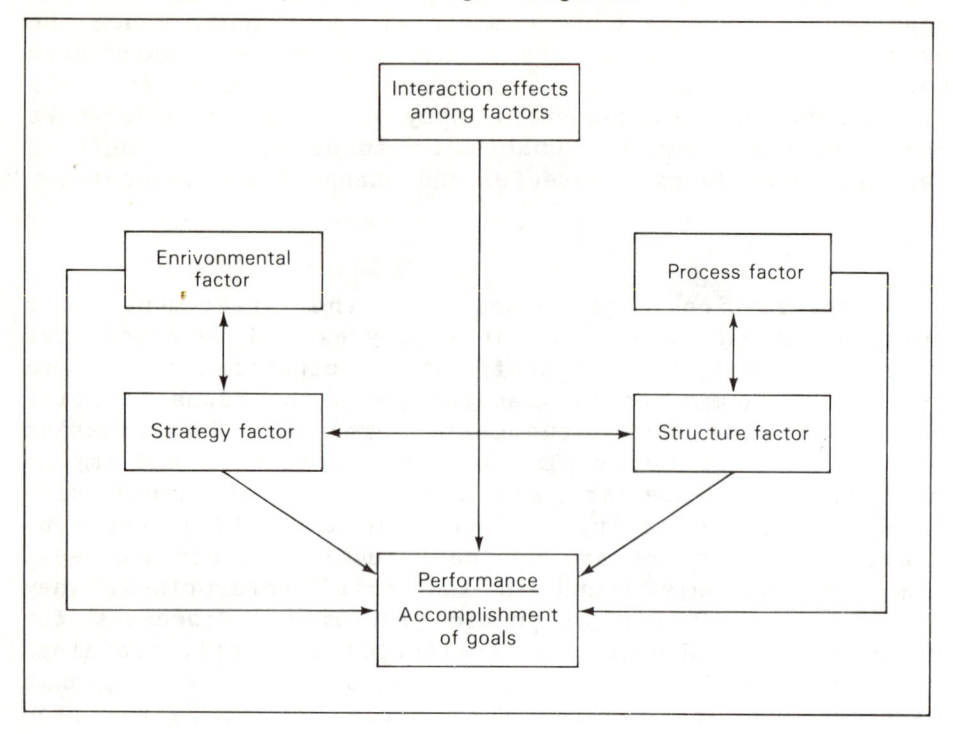

```
                    ┌──────────────────┐
                    │Interaction effects│
                    │  among factors    │
                    └──────────────────┘
                             │
    ┌──────────────┐                    ┌──────────────┐
    │ Enrivonmental│                    │Process factor│
    │    factor    │                    │              │
    └──────────────┘                    └──────────────┘
           ↕                                    ↕
    ┌──────────────┐                    ┌──────────────┐
    │Strategy factor│◄──────────────────►│Structure factor│
    └──────────────┘                    └──────────────┘
             \          ┌────────────┐          /
              \         │ Performance│         /
               ────────►│Accomplishment│◄─────
                        │  of goals   │
                        └────────────┘
```

(3) Programme managers can influence, modify and match them to improve programme performance.

A schema of how these factors interact and influence performance is shown in figure 4. In addition to these four factors, the diagram has a fifth box to represent the interaction effects among them.

3.2 <u>The concept of congruence</u>

Good farmers know how to apply several inputs such as seeds, water, fertiliser and cultural practices in the right proportions to obtain high yields. The right proportions vary from one crop to another and from one physical environment to another. A farmer also knows that while the quality of each input contributes to his crop yield, the right combination of inputs raises his yields more than any individual input alone does. Thus high yielding varieties of rice seeds are more productive than traditional varieties. But when these seeds are grown with the right dosages of water and fertilisers, yields tend to be much higher than when these inputs are missing or inadequate. For example, if fertiliser is not applied, these varieties will yield very little. Similarly, if fertiliser is applied without simultaneously providing adequate water, then again, productivity will be low. Different inputs can thus reinforce each other to yield increased outputs. There is a "synergy" in the combination that no single input alone can generate. Much of the high yield is therefore attributed to this synergy. Many examples of synergy are found in the fields of technology and industrial production also.[1]

Synergy is vital to good strategic management. The four factors work together to make strategic management powerful and effective. For them to work together, they must be consistent with one another very much as seeds, water and fertiliser reinforce one another in crop production. We call this phenomenon of mutual consistency "congruence". Performance of a development programme improves when there is "congruence" among environment, strategy, structure and process. No arbitrary combination of these is likely to yield good results. For example, a small farmer development strategy that does not effectively cope with the uncertainty of weather or markets in the farmers' environment cannot succeed. On the other hand, a strategy that guarantees reasonable prices to farmers or provides marketing support is likely to attract farmers. Given such uncertainty and variations between different areas, a rigid, centralised organisational structure that gives extension personnel little freedom to adapt will perform poorly. If extension staff must adapt to changing local conditions, and the internal organisational processes for training and motivating them are weak, then again, there will be no congruence between such internal processes and other factors and the programme will again perform poorly. Planning and integration are required so that the four basic factors work together.

3.3 <u>Top management's role</u>

Programme managers' critical role is to influence en-

---

[1] We have earlier used the term "interaction effects" to signify synergy effects. Economists use the term "production function" to represent the relationship between output and its underlying input combination.

vironment, strategy, structure and process to create a state of congruence among them. Then the programme will benefit from the synergy that flows as these factors reinforce each other. Sometimes programmes succeed solely because their environments are favourable or their political support is strong, but most programme leaders can succeed only when they consciously create and maintain congruence among the key factors.

In private enterprises, top managers are always expected to do this. If they do not, market competition ruthlessly eliminates them. The market test is so powerful that strategic management must be seriously practised by private enterprises. Perhaps this explains why the concept itself was developed in the context of business enterprises. Most of the literature and experience on this subject has been confined to the business world. Public sector organisations tend to survive and even grow, irrespective of their performance. This is partly why political leaders and public managers seldom give priority to strategic management.

Development programme managers rarely receive a mandate to practise strategic management and achieve congruence among the four factors. In chapter 2, we highlighted three constraints on public managers. Governments tend to impose multiple and often conflicting programme goals, resources are seldom sufficient and the goals-means orchestration is limited in public organisations. These constraints make it difficult to practise strategic management in development programmes. On the other hand, for the same reason, every effort should be made to analyse and influence the four factors as much as one can. When you carefully analyse the environment and the different constraints, new strategic or structural interventions suggest themselves. This, in turn, enables the programme manager to achieve congruence among the different factors. Here are three examples of such adaptive interventions:

(1) Though governments tend to prescribe multiple objectives and services for development programmes, successful programme managers often begin with only one dominant goal or service. As they gain experience and credibility, they take up other goals. Alternatively, when several goals are to be pursued simultaneously, they

choose closely related goals or services, and not unrelated ones. The managers of the National Dairy Development Programme of India focused first on milk, even though their programme agency had multiple objectives. They subsequently diversified into oilseed development after a decade when they had stabilised their dairy development mission. Indonesia's successful Population Programme concentrated first on family planning and took up nutrition as a service after it had built up an effective family planning service. In Kenya, though the Government had initially set up a new programme agency to develop five different crops for African small farmers, it permitted the agency to focus on tea, thus modifying its original mandate for the programme.[1] In fact, growing evidence supports the view that if top programme managers can evolve strategies to achieve goals sequentially in view of the environmental problems facing them, reasonable governments will support such strategic adaptations.

(2) When hierarchical structures, common in government, are slow and unwieldy, some programme managers have successfully turned to local communities to perform selected tasks. Sometimes, private markets and channels have delivered certain inputs or services which had been delivered less efficiently by government agencies. In China's public health programme, the population was mobilised in preventive campaigns to fight environmental and parasitic diseases. The barefoot doctors who served the rural areas were farmers or workers who worked part time to provide health services. In a rural education programme in Mexico, small rural communities were given the responsibility to build modest schools and feed and house their young instructors. The programme agency also stayed small and compact by subcontracting services and expert inputs to perform programme tasks.

(3) Several successful development programmes follow careful phasing strategies. In view of their complex environment and limitations of structure and manpower, they cover selected areas of the country first and gradually extend their services to other parts. Simultaneous expan-

---

[1] Programme managers may sometimes have more flexibility in these matters than they realise. Some people simply do not take advantage of their opportunities.

sion all over a large country would have imposed heavy strains on their structures. Such strategic adaptations contribute to congruence. India's Dairy Development Programme covered the country in two phases. Indonesia's Population Programme was implemented in three phases.

3.4 Points to remember

The major points that programme managers should bear in mind about strategic management are:

1. Strategic management is the set of top management interventions which provides the framework for all operational decisions and actions and hence facilitates effective performance.

2. Programme managers should monitor and influence four key factors in order to practise strategic management; these are the programme's external environment, strategy, structure and internal processes.

3. Since these factors interact, congruence among them is a pre-requisite for improving performance. The individual impact of the different factors as well as their interaction can be influenced by managers.

4. The programme leader's critical role is to analyse, influence and orchestrate these factors to achieve the best results. By orchestration, we mean the achievement of consistency among the factors.

5. Whenever the programme environment or objectives change, management should realign the factors. Thus, orchestration is not a one-time task; programme leaders must continually monitor changes among the four factors and orchestrate them when necessary.

READING THE ENVIRONMENT 4

The environment of a development programme is the set of external forces that influence its outcome. When a programme is limited to a small area or region of a country, the local or regional environment may have a stronger influence on its performance than does the national environment. If a programme's activities are affected by international developments either on the output or input side (e.g. international markets, aid prospects, etc.), then trends in the international environment may influence its performance. The nature and scope of the environment relevant to a development programme depends largely on the programme's objectives and scope, sectoral focus, and spatial coverage and linkages. Environments and programmes interact dynamically. A programme to develop a single crop, for example, has a more limited environment than a programme for multiple crops. A programme to integrate multiple inputs (e.g. seeds, fertilisers, extensions, water and credit) must interact with more organisations and actors than one which only provides extension or credit. A programme covering the entire country has a more complex environment than a regional programme. Sometimes, the large size of a country or an unfavourable environment leads policy makers to limit a programme's goals.

4.1 The role of environmental analysis

Most programme managers agree that "reading" the environment is important, but very few clearly understand how to go about this complex business. In the business world, managers can more easily monitor certain key environmental indicators or trends. Market prices, compet-

43

itors' outputs, growth of national income, etc., are data on the environment which may be readily available. Managers of development programmes should similarly look for data and signals in the environment which can assist them in making important strategic decisions. Reading the environment is essential for both strategic, long-term decisions as well as tactical, short-term decisions. We discuss below five areas which require important inputs from the environment.

(1) Diagnosis of the problems of the sector or services.

(2) Identification of the programme's beneficiaries and clients.

(3) Demand for the programme's services.

(4) Supply of the programme's services.

(5) Key actors influencing demand and supply.

Diagnosis of the problems of the sector or services

The basic data and insights on the key problems of the sector served by a development programme can be generated only from that programme's environment. Possibly in formulating a national development plan, these sectors have been analysed. However, the problems and gaps identified in a macro exercise are unlikely to be adequate for the design of a specific development programme. A programme needs a well-defined output or service. To make it effective, the elements that make up the service and linkages must be determined by analysing the problems in the environment. In an agricultural programme, several inputs (seeds, water, fertiliser, etc.) may have to be provided to the farmer simultaneously in order to increase crop yields. Whether all of these need to be provided by the programme, however, can be ascertained only by a careful analysis of the environment. Possibly farmers can generate some inputs themselves. Alternatively, private channels may exist to do this effectively.

Programme designs imported or developed with inadequate environmental analyses usually fail. A realistic design or concept of service can be generated only by carefully diagnosing the problems and gaps in the environment. A major reason for undertaking pilot projects is to assist in this diagnostic and design function.

Identification of beneficiaries and clients

Environmental analysis can enable the programme authority to understand and focus on relevant client groups. Though the programme objectives enunciated by the Government may specify the broad beneficiary and client groups, detailed analysis will be required to identify and segment the beneficiaries into homogenous groups. Many programmes implicitly assume all beneficiaries to be alike. A smallscale industry development programme, for example, may define its client, the small entrepreneur, as one who starts an industrial venture with an investment below a specified limit (e.g. US$ one million). A standard service is then provided to all clients based on the assumption that all these entrepreneurs need identical services. In fact, nothing could be farther from the truth. An urban entrepreneur with education and experience may need quite different services from those needed by a new rural entrepreneur. Location, skills, infrastructure, and type of industry are some criteria by which entrepreneurs could be segmented. This analysis may well lead to the conclusion that providing the same service to these diverse groups will not yield the desired results.

Beneficiary or client groups are part of the environment of the development programme. A programme is effective only to the extent that its benefits reach the intended beneficiaries. The diagnosis of problems discussed above is closely intertwined with the client focus of the programme. Base line studies, market surveys, etc., are used to assess the basic characteristics of beneficiaries and their changing needs. Continuous monitoring of the clientele is an essential part of environmental analysis as changes over time may have impiications for the strategic interventions of the programme.

A sector's problems can be analysed while ignoring the question of who benefits from the programme. When an agricultural programme focuses on a crop, the techno-economic inputs needed for its development dominate the design of the programme service. It will be assumed that all farmers will follow the advice of the programme's field staff. If the farmers are a heterogenous lot, this approach reflects a failure to perceive important available information. A proper reading of the environment helps the programme manager to segment the farmers into groups and consider the strategic question of whether all segments should be served at once or provided the same service, especially if the diagnosis of the problems of the sector reveal considerable diversity.

Consider an agricultural programme which offers farmers only high quality seeds and extension. Farmers who respond to this programme are likely to be those who on their own can obtain the remaining inputs. They can buy their own fertilisers, get water for irrigation, and raise investment funds. But, if the farmers differ in terms of income and farm size, many farmers may fail to find these inputs on their own. Thus smaller and poorer farmers may need special assistance which the first set of farmers did not need. Questions about diversity among the beneficiaries and the need for offering different types of services can be answered only through a process of careful environmental analysis.

Demand for the programme's service

Managers of many development programmes assume that demand exists for the programme's outputs or services. They seldom ask why clients should use these services or what could be done to improve public response. This attitude does not create major problems as long as demand exists for the programme's output.[1] When demand is poor, services are offered, but public response is poor.

Analysing the environment helps one solve a programme's demand problem. Barriers as well as support may be found in the political, economic, socio-cultural or technological dimensions of the environment. In the Indian dairy development programme, the urban cattle keepers and milk traders were politically strong and did not wish to see rural milk co-operatives grow. The Indonesian family

---

[1] This happens often in economic programmes. Enough entrepreneurs or farmers may be aware of the benefits and willing to respond to some programmes. If supply is extremely limited, then again, the same phenomenon may occur.

planning programme recognised early that an important environmental barrier was the socio-cultural attitudes of people towards fertility control. Religious leaders opposed the programme. The Indian dairy programme managers found that the technological improvements introduced by the railways to facilitate long-distance haulage and refrigeration favoured the setting up of rural refrigerating plants away from the cities, and thereby elicited a more positive response from small dairy farmers in rural areas. Many crop development programmes have found that response to their services is poor when farmers face severe economic risks due to uncertain weather.

These examples reinforce the importance of scanning the political, economic, socio-cultural and technological forces in a programme's environment. Creative strategies for harnessing the positive forces and minimising the effects of the negative forces will be thought of in the scanning process. Technical specialists who design programmes often tend to overlook or ignore how these forces can affect the demand for programme services.

Pilot projects are one means of testing the strength of demand for a development programme. Extrapolating from the experience of pilot projects, however, may be misleading, especially when the larger national environment differs significantly from the local environment of the pilot project. More systematic ways to assess the forces operating in the national environment and setting up several pilot projects in different parts of the country are some of the approaches programme managers might consider when going national.

<u>Supply of the programme's service</u>

Though "supply" or "service delivery" is the focus of many development programmes, few programme managers and designers know enough about the implications of environmental factors for their supply function. Mechanistic or standardised approaches to the design and delivery of services work well when the environment is reasonably homogenous in terms of clientele, physical conditions, logistics, etc. As a programme expands in size and geographical coverage, these features usually change. It is extremely important, therefore, for programme managers to search for the following features which may have a direct impact on their supply tasks.

(1) <u>The degree of diversity in the environment</u>: When there are heterogeneous groups of clients or beneficiaries in the country, the supply system must take this into account if supply and demand are to match properly. Problems and requirements may differ from one group to another and also over time due to cultural or social backgrounds, experience, etc., or to physical and geographical factors which make differences between regions significant.

(2) <u>Problems of logistics</u>: The quantity and quality of transport, storage and communications vary a great deal from country to country. Environmental analysis helps us assess the adequacy of facilities and skills before planning the supply strategy.

(3) <u>Adequacy of institutions</u>: Programmes which do not completely control production and delivery systems must carefully investigate the strengths and weaknesses of the institutions with which they must collaborate. These choices have strategic implications. The larger the size and coverage of the programme, the more critical the analysis of collaborating institutions.

<u>Key actors influencing demand and supply</u>

The environment includes not only impersonal forces and features which influence programme performance, but also actors who can affect the demand for and supply of the programme's service. We have highlighted the beneficiaries or clients who are important key actors to be influenced by programme managers. There are also important political, economic, socio-cultural and technological actors who can affect the demand or supply sides of the programme. In the Indonesian population programme, religious leaders were important actors whom the programme managers had to influence. Some actors, like political leaders and senior officials in the Government, play a key role in supporting or defeating a programme's strategy. Some may determine the amount of resources a programme could receive from the Government or other sources. They thus influence the programme's ability to supply its service. Local community leaders may have considerable influence on the response of clients to a programme. Search for and identification of the key actors of a programme calls for a good understanding of the different segments of the society. An important reason for reading the environment is to be close to the key actors who influence the forces of demand and supply of the programme, and to mobilise their support.

The foregoing dimensions are important for assessing the complexity of the environment. Strategic interventions must be based on the degree of environmental complexity. Given extreme complexity, programme managers should limit the programme goals and services until they are adequately familiar with the environment. When the environment is complex, programme expansion should proceed with cautioun. These assessments will vary as conditions change. An analysis of the environment can facilitate the strategic choices of any development programme. These strategic choices will be discussed in detail in the next chapter.

4.2 Scope, diversity and uncertainty

The preceding section discussed the size of the programme, the diversity among client groups and uncertainty about public response. These examples illustrate the impact of the environment on the programme.[1] It is useful, therefore, to examine these basic dimensions systematically and to understand how they could be integrated into an exercise in environmental analysis.

Scope

The size or spatial coverage of a development programme usually tells us something about the "scope" of its environment. Pilot projects, for example, serve limited areas and need not reckon with complex national environments. A programme which deals with one crop or commodity has a more limited environment than a multi-crop programme or a programme which attempts to integrate agriculture with social services. The size of the programme is not an adequate index of the scope of its environment.

The identification and diagnosis of a sector's problems are more complex when a programme's environment is

---

[1] Organisational theorists have analysed a variety of environment properties and their implications for organisational structure. See J. Galbraith: <u>Organisation design</u> (Reading, Massachusetts, Addison-Wesley, 1977).

wide (e.g. when a project expands into a national programme). Mobilising demand is more difficult when the scope of its environment gets progressively wider. Generally speaking, environmental complexity tends to be directly related to the dimension of scope. A strategic response is to sequence the programme in space and time. For instance, a new programme may be first implemented in one region and later extended to the rest of the country in phases.

Diversity

A programme's environment is rarely homogenous. Its physical-geographic features, and economic and socio-political characteristics are usually diverse. These and other historical forces create considerable diversity among the beneficiaries or clients and the terrain where the programme operates. Environmental analysis should thus search for homogenous client groups or homogenous clusters of these features to support decisions about our five strategic areas. When the environment is diverse, a programme should provide differentiated services to the diverse groups rather than a standardised service for all. Failure to generate and utilise such insights causes serious problems for large agricultural programmes and in social services such as education. When a standardised service fails to meet client needs, the problem manifests itself in a fall in demand or public response to the programme. The greater the diversity, the more complex the environment of the programme.

Uncertainty

Environments are seldom stable. Changeable weather patterns greatly influence farmers' behaviour and responses to a programme. Changes in political conditions influence the strategy a programme should adopt. Changes in the perception of clients or their dissatisfaction with a service can significantly change their response to a programme. Even rumours in the village can upset the response to sensitive nutrition or family planning programmes. Environments vary in the degree of uncertainty underlying their political, economic, and social conditions. When changes are frequent and unpredictable, the programme strategies should be flexible. Participation of beneficiaries or clients in the design and delivery of services, increased autonomy of field staff at the grass roots to enable them to adapt to emerging situations, and forging of close linkages with key factors in the environment are good strategies for programme managers confronted by uncertain environments.

The analysis of environmental uncertainty should consider each of the five areas discussed above. Strategic responses should vary depending on whether problems arise from uncertainty, diversity or scope. To illustrate, diverse client needs may call for differentiated services. Uncertain client response may call for client participation or the use of strong economic incentives. Wide scope may call for indirect ways of mobilising clients (e.g. mass communication, use of a network of institutions, etc.), since direct control of, or contact with, a nationwide clientele may be infeasible. These responses have important implications for the structural and process interventions of programme which we shall deal with in subsequent chapters.

Scope, diversity and uncertainty do not necessarily move together. If the environment is homogenous, a programme may expand its scope with no serious problems posed by diversity. Economic or political uncertainty may be high, irrespective of the scope or diversity of an environment. In short, environmental complexity increases as uncertainty along these three dimensions increases. They share no common scale. Their usefulness lies in the analytical insights they offer towards understanding the environment in which development programmes operate.

Some illustrations may make these ideas clearer. Japan is a large country (scope); yet the people are remarkably homogenous in language and culture. A much smaller country such as Uganda may have greater diversity because of traditional tribal and other differences and the disparities between urban and rural areas and high and low income groups. Sometimes, environmental diversity may be low, but uncertainty of market or climatic conditions may be high. Most Philippine farmers are small operators (low diversity), but fluctuations in weather conditions and consequently in market prices and profits creates considerable environmental uncertainty.

4.3 Search for information

Since it is difficult to assess these dimensions and their impact on the five strategic areas through an abstract analysis or desk research, many development programmes adopt pilot projects to help them understand the environment. The problems of a sector or service, the nature of the client group, and issues relevant to the demand for and supply of the service can be better appreciated through pilot projects. If it is likely that scope, diversity and uncertainty will pose problems, pilot projects or experiments may be organised in different parts of the country and under varying conditions. When the environment is complex, a "live" analysis of this type can be valuable. When a programme is extended to cover a large region, the insights gained from the different experiments must be fed into the design of strategic and structural interventions.

Pilot projects, however, do not help us assess some segments of the environment. For example, since a pilot project is usually located in a small area, the potential impact of political forces and pressures on the programme when it covers the country cannot be gauged from the pilot experience. Problems of logistics and supply cannot be easily extrapolated from pilot project experience. On the other hand, the techno-economic insights gained from pilot projects may be relevant to all parts of the country. Additional evidence on certain segments of the environment may therefore need to be gathered when pilot projects are scaled up and the scope of the environment is widened. Specialised surveys of the relevant population and leaders, demand studies, analysis of national networks and channels of distribution, etc., are some techniques used to obtain supplementary information.

The limitations of pilot projects highlight the need for a careful analysis of the <u>different segments of the environment</u>, each of which may have both positive and negative features. Though the segments relevant to different programmes vary, it is advisable to scan all major <u>political</u>, <u>economic</u>, <u>technological</u> and <u>socio-cultural</u> segments of the environment. Opportunities as well as threats to the programme could be identified by examining each segment in relation to the five strategic areas. Problems posed by scope, diversity and uncertainty may exist in all segments.

Figure 5 A simple framework for environmental analysis

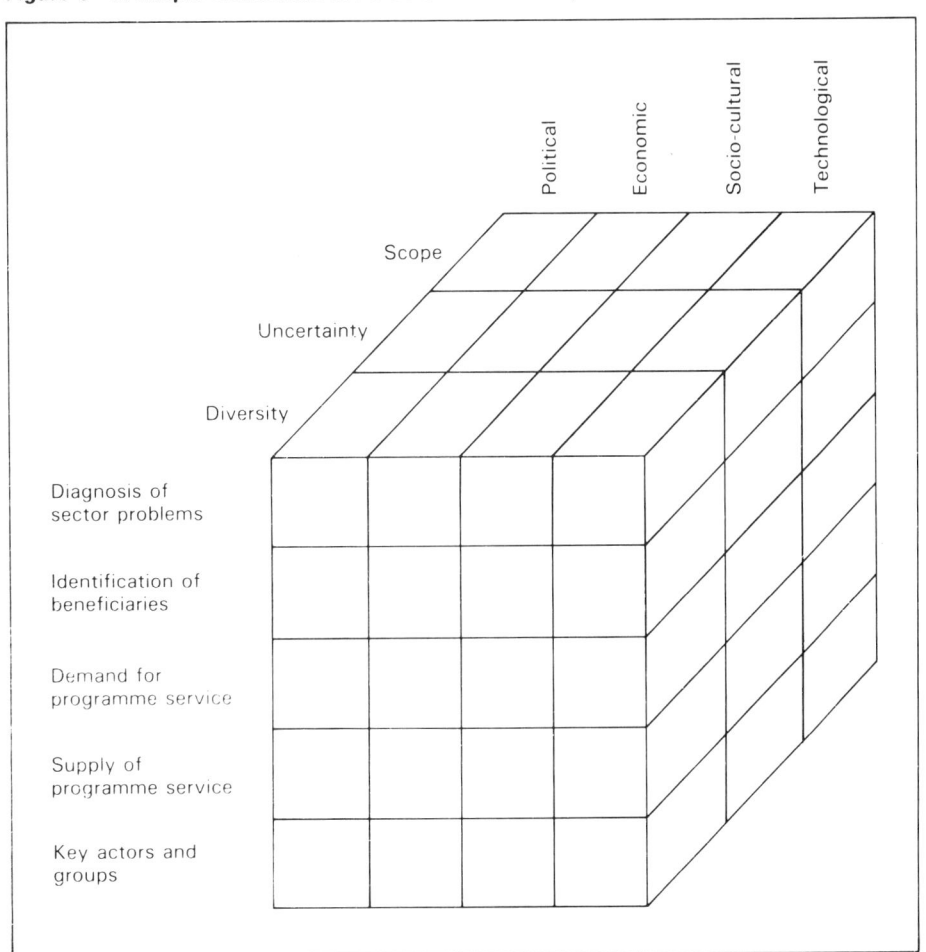

[Figure 5: A three-dimensional cube diagram. The top axis shows segments: Political, Economic, Socio-cultural, Technological. The depth axis shows: Scope, Uncertainty, Diversity. The vertical axis (left side) shows strategic areas: Diagnosis of sector problems, Identification of beneficiaries, Demand for programme service, Supply of programme service, Key actors and groups.]

Environmental analysis is a three dimensional exercise. We need inputs from the environment to enable programme managers to make the best decisions in each of the five <u>strategic areas</u>. The <u>different segments</u> of the environment must be investigated to generate the inputs relevant to each strategic areas. In the process of this investigation, the problems posed by <u>scope, diversity and uncertainty</u> in each segment and their likely impact on the strategic areas must be identified. Figure 5 depicts the relationships among these three dimensions.

The search for environmental information and insights can be better focused with the aid of figure 5. Take the first strategic area "diagnosis of sector problems". The horizontal cells call for an analysis of environmental

53

data from each of the relevant segments of the environment. The cells above this row emphasise the need to examine each of the environmental segments from the standpoint of the dimensions of scope, diversity and uncertainty. The relative importance of segments and dimensions may vary from one programme to another. But the general framework is useful for all.

The Indonesian population programme illustrates this framework for environmental analysis. In the strategic area of "diagnosis of sector problems", it was important to consider the influence of religious leaders and other local elders hostile to the programme. This was a socio-political factor. There was some diversity among the leaders as there were two groups, the Muslim majority and the Hindu minority. The potential hostility of leaders meant that public response was uncertain. This factor was not limited to any one area and was therefore national in scope. The military regime was also a political factor. Both were relevant inputs in evolving the programme strategy.

The economic effects of population pressure could be easily identified. On the other hand, there would be no immediate and visible gains to the people from fertility control. This had implications for the motivation of the public. In perceiving gains, urban and rural people might differ (diversity). There was more uncertainty about the likely response of rural people. Again the scope of this economic factor was national.

In the socio-cultural area, village communities were highly structured and local leaders had considerable authority over rural people. Similarly, religious objections to surgical operations for fertility control was a factor. The influence of these factors extended across the country and response to the programme was certain to be negative if they were ignored.

Some technologies for fertility control were more strongly resisted than others. Use of technologies more consistent with the environment (e.g. oral pills) was a response to this problem. The non-availability of medical facilities in villages was also a factor to be considered in the choice of technologies. Response to the programme could be made more certain by taking these factors into account.

A similar search for critical forces or factors needs to be undertaken to identify beneficiaries, demand for programme service, etc. This is a somewhat specialised exercise which goes beyond the scope of this book. However, this illustration, though brief, suggests how figure 5 could be used for planning a more systematic analysis of the environment in many programmes.

4.4 Guidelines for environmental analysis

Environmental analysis should be undertaken not merely when a programme is established, but throughout its life cycle. A standard format or a specific sequence of steps for analysis cannot therefore be prescribed to fit the needs of all programmes. A great deal of adaptation to the prevailing circumstances and the nature of the programme is called for whenever programme managers undertake this exercise. The general considerations for an environmental analysis are summarised below:

1. The starting point is a clear focus on the strategic areas or, for that matter, any major decision for which environmental data are being sought. The five areas discussed in this chapter may meet the needs of most development programmes. Managers should review these decision areas and make sure that they are relevant to their situation.

2. Analyse the different segments of the environment to identify and interpret both positive and negative factors and forces which may have an impact on each strategic area. A limited view of the environment (e.g. exclusive focus on technology or economic focus) may lead to the neglect of some environmental factors which may turn out to be critical later.

3. Analyse the dimensions of the environment such as scope, diversity and uncertainty. Since the impact of these dimensions is not uniform across all segments and decision areas, the search for data and insights may call for considerable specialised knowledge.

4. <u>Information on the environment</u> should be generated in a variety of ways using diverse sources. Initial project reports often contain valuable basic data. Surveys of specific sectors undertaken by the government or donor agencies may shed light on environmental conditions. On significant aspects, special field studies or experiments may be commissioned if no organised knowledge exists (e.g. demand studies, attitude surveys, demonstrations, etc.). Pilot projects are another major source of environmental data. Interactions with key actors in the environment can provide useful insights on the forces at work and likely changes in future. A variety of sources, both formal and informal, is a must precisely because no single source is likely to have access to the entire range of data being sought.

5. Since environments change over time, every programme should develop its own <u>system for monitoring ongoing developments</u> and <u>updating its stock of data</u>. In addition to specialised efforts, periodic reviews of developments by the top management with all those within the organisation who interact with the environment can play a useful role in the monitoring and updating process.

6. The approach presented in this chapter is designed to assist the programme manager in his search for relevant environmental data. The framework depicted in figure 5, which looks formidable and comprehensive, has value only to the extent that it enables the manager to ask the right questions. Both time constraints and paucity of data may prevent him from undertaking a comprehensive analysis in many a situation. However, even in the face of such constraints, he will be better off organising his data search with the aid of this framework than without it.

FORMULATING THE PROGRAMME STRATEGY   5

Technology generally dominates the strategies of development programmes. Technologists and other specialists tend to dominate design decisions. A common tendency is to concentrate on technology and ignore other aspects of design. Developing countries often import programme designs from abroad, without reference to the environments in which they are to implemented. In chapter 4, we explored the different ways in which a country's environment influences programme performance. These influences are not limited to technology, but include economic and political factors and the attributes of beneficiaries. These cannot be analysed or understood through any single discipline. Technology is important but not sufficient for strategic planning and implementation. In this chapter, we shall discuss the building blocks of strategy formulation and demonstrate the need to pull together knowledge and insights from different sources and aspects of life and experience. Strategic thinking is a "synthetic" effort and cannot be left to any single group of specialists. Top programme leaders and managers must actively participate in this process.

5.1 The basic influences on strategy

Strategy is the set of long-term choices about the operating goals, policies and action plans of a programme. Two important factors influence these choices. The <u>objectives</u> laid down by government and the <u>environment</u> of the programme will influence the strategy. Few programme strategies take these factors adequately into account. Programme performance suffers when they are ignored.

The objectives laid down by the government usually indicate a programme's direction. These objectives provide a basis for choosing among strategic alternatives. If the goals of a programme do not fit the objectives of the government, the programme leaders will find it difficult to get resources and support. Since government seldom spells out the goals specifically, the programme leadership can choose its operating goals with some flexibility. If, on the other hand, a government is specific about a single objective, flexibility is limited. Even then, there may be considerable scope for choosing between alternative ways to achieve an objective.

For example, when the National Dairy Development Board of India was set up, the broad objectives given to it included not only the development of dairy farming, but also fisheries and other agricultural activities. Yet the operating goals of the Board in its initial years included only dairy development. This choice was consistent with the objectives of the Government of India, but did not include all the objectives laid down by the Government. Small industry development programmes in many countries tend to focus on certain areas and industries. Yet the original objectives set for them may show that they were intended to cater to all areas and all kinds of industries. Some programmes cover this vast ground in several phases, not all at once. Strategic choices thus help managers to be consistent with the objectives given by their governments without being overwhelmed by them.

Strategy cannot be formulated without reference to the programme's environment. The dimensions of the environment were described in the preceding chapter. Governments commonly pay lip service to these dimensions, but then adopt imported designs without questioning their relevance to the local environment. Consequently, programmes fail and scarce resources are wasted. When diversity and uncertainty are severe, a strategy which ignores the environment cannot succeed. When an environment's complexity increases, the strategic choices must reflect this. Similarly, the more complex the objectives of a programme, the greater the attention to be paid to its strategy. When conflicting and multiple objectives are to be achieved, strategic choices become increasingly difficult. Under these conditions, programme leaders tend to reduce complexity by limiting their goals.

They can phase the accomplishment of multiple goals by first focusing on a <u>dominant</u> goal. The simultaneous pursuit of diverse goals requires the management of diverse services or outputs leading to a severe organisational overload. The conflicts and the mounting demands on the time and skills of top management then spells disaster for the programme. Only through a careful analysis of the complexity of objectives given by the government and the complexity of the environment can the operating goals of the programme be determined. This is the first and basic strategic choice that faces a development programme.[1]

> For example, the National Food and Agriculture Council of the Philippines was charged with developing several crops such as rice and corn, and fisheries and fruits and vegetables. The Government, in fact, had given multiple objectives and tasks to this organisation. To achieve these simultaneously would have meant creating a huge multi-service programme covering the whole country. It would certainly have taxed the Council and its limited skills and manpower. The environment was complex. Weather, market prices and responses of farmers were all uncertain. Each crop or subsector required special attention to the unique inputs needed for its development. The problem, however, was most severe for rice, the country's staple food. With the Government's explicit support, the Council therefore decided to focus on the achievement of self-sufficiency in rice as a goal, deliberately giving less attention and resources to other crops. This was clearly a case of choosing a <u>dominant operating goal</u>, and assigning lower priority to the objectives given by the Government in relation to other sub-sectors. The intention was to reduce complexity by first focusing on a single or dominant goal and <u>sequentially</u> moving towards other goals. It was the careful attention given to the environment and the objectives laid down by the Government that led the programme leadership to this strategic choice of a dominant operating goal.

---

[1] This behaviour has been observed in the context of firms. See H.A. Simon and J. March: <u>Organisation</u> (New York, Wiley, 1958) and R. Cyert and J. March: <u>The behavioural theory of the firm</u> (New York, Prentice Hall, 1973).

The choice of operating goals is merely the starting point of strategy formulation. In order to be useful guides to action, these goals need to be spelt out in detail and the major tasks which flow from them should be identified. There are two sets of components which are influenced by the operating goals. We shall call them <u>service-beneficiary-sequence</u> (SBS) strategy and <u>demand-supply-resource</u> (DSR) strategy. The former is concerned more with <u>goals</u> and the latter with <u>tasks</u>. They are interdependent building blocks in so far as goals influence the scope of tasks and the complexity of tasks in turn affects the scope of goals. We have separated them into two sets for a better understanding of their roles. In reality, they are merely different dimensions of the same phenomenon that we called strategy. The linkages among the building blocks may be seen in figure 6. The six components of SBS and DSR hang together as we shall explain below.

5.2 The service-beneficiary-sequence (SBS) strategy

Three questions must be asked in formulating a programme strategy:

(1) What is the service or output of the programme?

(2) For whom is it developed?

(3) When is the service to be provided?

The goals of a programme are achieved through the services it provides. The concept of the programme service therefore is an important dimension of strategy. The content of the service must meet the needs of the beneficiaries. The question, <u>for whom</u>, is critical, though those who view programme design narrowly seldom ask or answer it. The third question concerns the time sequence (<u>when</u>) of service delivery. The answer depends on the nature of the service as well as the complexity of the environment.

Every programme offers some output or service to its beneficiaries. We use the term "service" since few programmes offer physical outputs or products. Physical inputs and the manner in which they are integrated are part of the service. What the people finally receive is a service. Thus, in the Indian Dairy Development Programme, though the focus is on a physical commodity, milk, the

Figure 6 The building blocks of strategy

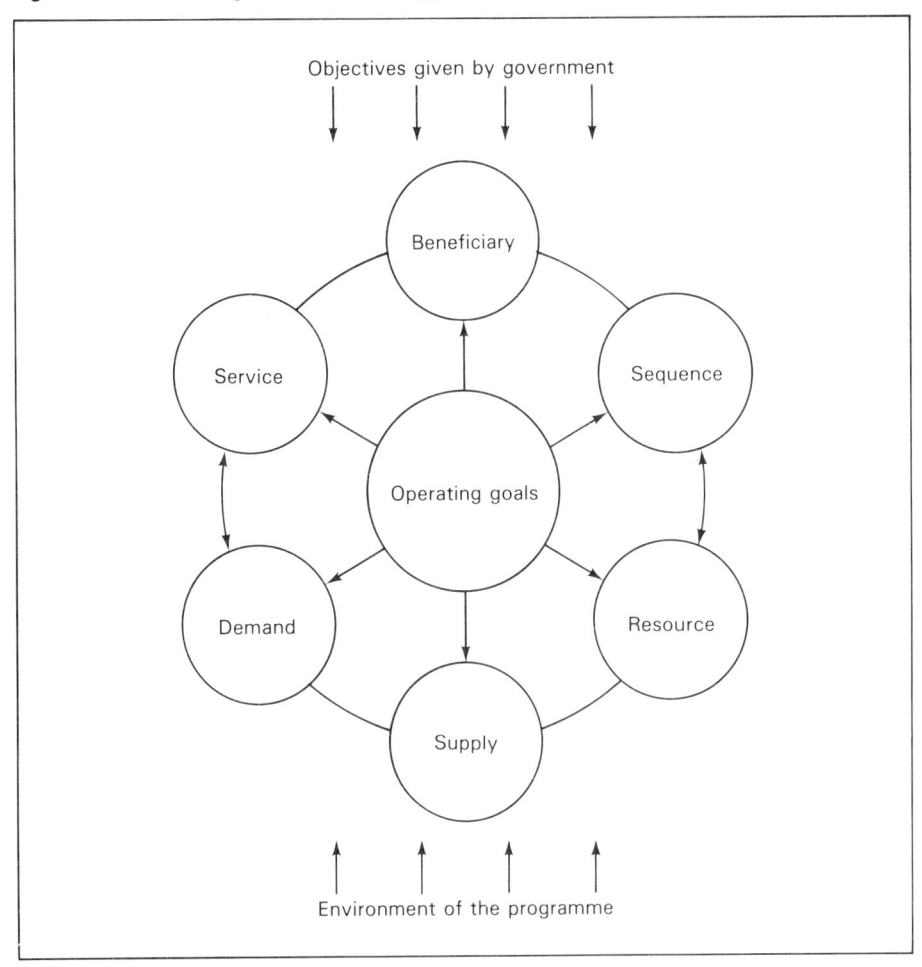

```
                    Objectives given by government
                      ↓    ↓    ↓    ↓

                           ┌─────────────┐
                           │ Beneficiary │
                           └─────────────┘
              ┌─────────┐                   ┌──────────┐
              │ Service │                   │ Sequence │
              └─────────┘                   └──────────┘
                           ┌─────────────┐
                           │ Operating   │
                           │   goals     │
                           └─────────────┘
              ┌─────────┐                   ┌──────────┐
              │ Demand  │                   │ Resource │
              └─────────┘                   └──────────┘
                           ┌─────────────┐
                           │   Supply    │
                           └─────────────┘

                      ↑    ↑    ↑    ↑
                    Environment of the programme
```

programme's service consists of the provision of a set of interrelated activities such as assistance in milk production, procurement, processing and marketing which help farmers to increase milk production and earn higher incomes. Viewing the programme service as milk production is wrong. It is important to ask what the concept of service is so that a comprehensive view can be taken of what the programme does to assist the beneficiaries.

Integration of inputs

Many programmes offer services to compensate for the beneficiaries' inability to perform certain tasks on their own. In defining the programme service, it is useful to ask how it performs this role. If beneficiaries could easily buy the service or its components in the market and integrate the components themselves, there would be no need for the programme.

In most developing countries, agricultural inputs such as high yielding varieties, irrigation, fertilisers and new cultural practices are not readily available to all farmers. Even if available, few farmers, especially the small farmers, are likely to be able to integrate these inputs themselves. Their motivation to use new practices may be low because of uncertainty about crop prices. Private markets may not offer adequate, stable incentives to farmers. Under these conditions, an agricultural programme's service should be designed not only to offer these inputs individually, but also to integrate them. This is the rationale of the functional and vertical integration strategy found in some of the more successful agricultural programmes.

In Kenya's smallholder tea development programme, the Kenya Tea Development Authority not only integrated the supply of inputs such as tea stumps, extension, fertilisers and credit for the small farmer, but also integrated tea production, procurement, processing and marketing. The latter is an example of vertical integration while the former reflects functional integration at the farm level. India's Dairy Development Board first integrated the inputs needed to enhance milk production (veterinary care, artificial insemination, fodder and extension) and then added milk procurement, processing and marketing to create the necessary vertical linkages. It would have been difficult for small farmers with limited knowledge and bargaining power to establish these linkages on their own. Both the Kenyan and the Indian programmes had a strategy of integration that compensated for the inability of their beneficiaries to integrate inputs on their own.

Dimensions of service: multiplicity, relatednesss and measurability

A few programmes focus on a single service. Some offer multiple services because their goals are multiple. Multiple services may be related or unrelated. Inputs and outputs may be measurable or unmeasurable. These features complicate strategy formulation. It is useful therefore to examine them closely. Three dimensions of service need to be explored.

First, the programme's service may be <u>single</u> or <u>multiple</u>. The dimension is the <u>diversity</u> of services. When a programme focuses on a single crop, we regard it as a single service programme even though it integrates multiple inputs to provide this service. On the other hand, an integrated rural development programme concerned with the development of crops, health and education is providing multiple services. Each individual activity requires different types of services. Hence there is a <u>diversity of services</u> in an integrated rural development programme. Each service must integrate unique inputs. Thus if there are four different services, there will be four different combinations of inputs for the programme to manage. Multiple services assume considerable competence and leadership on the part of programme managers.

Second, multiple services may be <u>related</u> or <u>unrelated</u>. A programme concerned with two agricultural crops grown by the same farmers and requiring several common inputs (e.g. fertiliser, water, credit), is providing <u>related</u> services. The common elements in the services make their management relatively simple. It is more complex to manage the services of two unrelated crops. Such services are then <u>unrelated</u>. Integrating inputs for unrelated services is complex. A health strategy which combines curative care and preventive care provides related services. But when curative care and primary education are offered, we treat them as unrelated services. Their inputs are totally different. The beneficiaries are also likely to be different. Services are more related when their inputs and beneficiaries have more in common. When the services are unrelated, the problem of diversity is more severe.

A third dimension of service is the <u>measurability</u> of inputs and outcomes. If the inputs of a service as well as its outcome are measurable, management control is relatively easy. Where these are difficult to measure, monitoring and control become more difficult. Programmes with economic goals pass the test of measurability better than those with social goals. The outcome of a preventive health care strategy or adult education strategy is more difficult to measure and evaluate than that of a rice programme or an export promotion strategy. In some cases, programme inputs can be measured, but not their outcomes. This permits at least the monitoring of inputs, but not of the programme impact.

The three dimensions of <u>diversity, relatedness and measurability</u> of services have a direct bearing on programme strategy. When services are divers, unrelated and difficult to measure, the task of management can be made easier if the programme starts off with a single service and subsequently moves into other services. This is a means of reducing complexity. We call this the strategy of <u>sequential diversification</u>. Another means of reducing complexity is to choose <u>related</u> goals and services. If sequential diversification is impossible, then the second-best course is to provide related programme services. A third strategy is to measure inputs and outputs <u>indirectly</u> where measurability is a problem. A search for <u>surrogate measures</u> is initiated to cope with the problem of measurability. Examples of these different strategic interventions can be found in a variety of programmes.

> Sequential diversification has been used by several successful development programmes. The Indian Dairy Development Programme started with a single service that focused on milk for twelve years. Then it took up oil seeds development as an additional activity or service. The Indonesian Population Programme concentrated on family planning in the first decade, and then diversified into nutrition and other population activities. The Chinese Public Health Programme, which had multiple goals, emphasised two related services, curative care and preventive care. In the Indonesian Programme, the immediate impact of family planning was difficult to measure. The strategy, therefore, focused on the number of acceptors, their problems and the supplies and services delivered to them. These were surrogate measures, but useful for monitoring and control. Minimising non-measurability was a strategic intervention by programme leadership.

<u>Beneficiaries: the problem of diversity</u>

The service concept entails some implicit assumptions about the characteristics of programme beneficiaries. Some services are meant for the entire population of a country or region, e.g. health services, infrastructure facilities, etc. Others benefit certain segments of the population, e.g. farmers, small-scale entrepreneurs, etc. A programme often fails to elicit the relevant public response simply because the relevant analysis of the beneficiaries and of their needs was not adequate. Irrigation projects fail due to poor utilisation of water when they ignore the needs of different groups of farmers. The naive assumption that the delivery of water was a standardised service was proved wrong by farmers who wanted the delivery to be tailored to their differing needs, by time of day and day of the week, for example.

As programme size and geographical scope increase, diversity among beneficiaries also increases. The same service may not meet the needs of diverse groups of beneficiaries. For instance, family planning services for urban people may need to be very different from that for the rural public. Pilot projects are initiated in different regions of a country to understand variations to be built into the programme service to match the needs of different segments of the population. Even a simple service for significantly diverse beneficiaries may have to be <u>differentiated</u>. For example, a rice development programme in a country with diverse climatic and farmer characteristics must offer differentiated services. When the differentiation required is high, a strategic decision has to be made on whether separate programmes are required to cater to the needs of different groups of beneficiaries. Thus a small farmers' programme may be separately set up because the service required by them has to be significantly differentiated from the service offered to larger farmers, even though both groups cultivate the same crop. Water supply and sanitation services for rural communities are usually differentiated from those of urban centres. Thus, for example, the Philippines have established three water programme agencies: one for large municipalities, another for 600 small cities and another for thousands of rural communities.

Sequence: phasing over time and space

When the beneficiaries of the services are diverse and the scope of the environment is wide, it becomes necessary to plan implementation in phases. Though this may look obvious, many governments implement programmes to cover the country all at once without considering these problems. Programme failures arise from the lack of a strategy for sequential expansion. Even a phased expansion tends to be a response to financial constraints. It is seldom recognised that environmental complexity and service-beneficiary diversity are important reasons why careful phasing of the programme implementation should be built into the strategy itself. Expansion of programmes become unmanageable without careful phasing.

Phasing strategy is different from the sequential diversification of services discussed earlier. The latter may be regarded as adding on new goals or services which were not part of the programme to begin with. Phasing, on the other hand, is concerned with how a given service is to be implemented. To illustrate, the Indonesian Population Programme covered the country in three phases. In the first phase, it operated only in Java and Bali, which were the two most densely populated islands of the country. In the second phase, the programme extended to one set of the outer islands which were sparsely populated. In the third phase, the remaining islands were covered. Extending the programme to all three simultaneously would have over-burdened management. Abundance of funds does not necessarily eliminate the need to phase programe implementation. Sequential moves also help the programme to learn as it goes from one phase to the next, thus enhancing its ability to improve performance over time.

5.3 The demand-supply-resource (DSR) strategy

SBS brings the operational goals of a programme closer to action. Design of the service, focus on specified beneficiaries and the extension of the service to desired areas (geographical phasing) over time are critical steps in translating goals into action. DSR, on the other hand, calls for careful planning at the very inception of the programme. The two together provide the basis for designing the action plans of the programme.

DSR highlights three basic tasks (1) public response to a programme service (demand), (2) the task of delivering the service to the public (supply), and (3) mobilisation of resources for the programme through the key actors in the environment. The mix of these tasks differs from one programme to another. For example, in programmes which are more concerned with social services like preventive health care or adult literacy, mobilising public demand may turn out to be a more important task than in other programmes. Let us look at each of these tasks.

Demand mobilisation

Many development programmes are managed as supply systems with explicit recognition of the role of service delivery alone. When there is excess demand for certain services, this approach may be adequate. When imports are cut off, domestic enterprises can sell all their products even if they do not advertise or drum up demand. Faced with shortages, enterprises do well even when they do nothing about mobilising demand.

Every programme manager ought to probe the demand aspects of his service well before its design is frozen. In fact, an understanding of the needs of the beneficiaries and the factors influencing them assists him or her in adapting the service to the environment. Beneficiaries may fail to respond because of problems of either willingness or ability or both. There are different ways of responding to the demand problem depending on the difficulties facing the beneficiaries.

(1) If unwillingness to use a service is the constraint, information as well as incentives are useful for mobilising demand. Unwillingness may be due to ignorance. Dissemination of information and advice may stimulate demand. The adoption of new agricultural technology and practices by farmers is facilitated by an information and advisory service. If unwillingness is due to the low gains or benefits perceived by the people, the demand strategy may need to pay increased attention to incentives. For example, in programmes for agricultural crops, it is important to ask whether additional returns to farmers are adequate incentives for them to respond to the new strategies.

(2) Service may sometimes be adapted to the changing needs of beneficiaries. Standardised services may be inappropriate for beneficiaries who become increasingly

unwilling to respond. In nutrition and family planning, this a major problem. When such uncertainties exist, <u>participation of beneficiaries</u> in operational planning and implementation can mobilise demand. Participation makes the service more relevant to the needs and more adaptive to the environment of the beneficiaries. This, in turn, increases their motivation to respond.

(3) If beneficiaries cannot take advantage of a programme's service, information and participation will not fully improve response. Even a "free" service may extract indirect costs beyond their means. Few poor farmers and labourers can send their children to free primary schools because the children's earnings are too valuable to be exchanged for the uncertain, long-term gains from education. Under these conditions, <u>income generation</u> is a prerequisite for mobilising demand for education. As long as incomes do not cross a threshold, beneficiaries cannot and will not demand the services of certain types of programmes. Influencing income generation then becomes a strategic intervention.

(4) Sometimes, major institutional reforms are needed before response to a programme can occur. Land reform, for example, may be a condition for tenant farmers to invest in agriculture and adopt new technologies. Such reforms seldom take place without the use of <u>power</u> through the government or people's own organisations. The ability of farmers to respond to the agricultural programme increases when they own land.

Both income generation and the use of power entail complex strategic interventions. Programme managers must examine closely the twin aspects of willingness and ability of beneficiaries and choose the most appropriate mix of interventions. The four types of interventions explained above merely offer broad guidelines to facilitate this choice.

<u>Supply</u>

Technology-intensive programmes tend to emphasise supply while ignoring demand. Irrigation projects which ignore water utilisation, and agricultural programmes which put their faith in miracle seeds and forget the farmer's other requirements are examples. Supply should be closely linked to the demand side of the programme. Three strategic considerations, which govern the supply task, are differentiation, pilot testing and efficiency.

First, it is important to analyse the degree of differentiation needed in the programme service to match the diversity in the needs of beneficiaries. A nutrition programme operating in diverse geographical regions may have to differentiate its service to suit the needs of beneficiaries in different regions. If the programme diversifies into family planning and health, similar differentiation may be necessary in these services too. The complexity of managing the supply of these widely differentiated and multiple services will be enormous.

Second, learning from the pilot project is an important aid to the supply task. Testing out production and delivery of service is facilitated by pilot projects. How to integrate the lessons of pilot experiences into the replication of the service should be a major concern of the supply strategy.

Third, efficiency of service delivery is low in many programmes. Special attention to keeping adequate supplies of inputs and organising logistics is required to avoid shortages so common in developing countries. Strategic planning rather than purely ad hoc moves are needed to ensure efficient service delivery. A programme may make use of public as well as private channels for service delivery.

Mobilisation of resources

Programme designers commonly think of resources in financial terms alone. However, resources, including funds, are often mobilised with the support of a variety of key actors in the government. They may be political or administrative leaders, and others who hold sway over potential beneficiaries, and agencies whose co-operation could make some difference to programme performance, e.g. religious leaders, local elders, heads of local governments, etc. These key actors may be persons and groups capable of influencing a programme either on the demand or supply side or both. Thus, building external linkages is a key function of the top management in many programmes. Designs on paper amount to little without a strategy for mobilising key actors whose support is essential to implementation. Identification of key actors and of the kinds of resources (resolution of conflicts, funds, facilitating public acceptance, etc.) they can provide, is a strategic task of programme managers.

In the Indonesian Population Programme, the intial emphasis was on the dissemination of information and advice as the primary means of mobilising public response. Soon when it was found that demand was not growing, the programme leaders hit upon the idea that an active role of the village communities in planning and implementation might create greater interest in the programme service. Participation of beneficiaries thus became an important instrument of demand mobilisation. Supply was organised to match demand for the service being created. It was recognised very early that logistics could prove a major hindrance to the timely delivery of the service in rural areas. The strategic decision to maintain liberal stocks of contraceptives on a decentralised basis and the flexible funding procedures used to obtain foreign aid to import and distribute these supplies reflect interventions to strengthen the supply task. An example of mobilising resources through key actors is the programme's careful strategy to win the support of the religious leaders and village elders for family planning.

The demand, supply and resource components of the programme strategy are clearly derived from the operating goals and the service-beneficiary-sequence components discussed earlier in this chapter. However, feedback from DSR may also help to modify and fine-tune the SBS strategy. Thus, if demand mobilisation is expected to be very difficult, it may well be reflected in the phasing strategy or decisions about beneficiary groups. SBS and DSR are, therefore, interdependent and must be treated as different parts which hang together. No programme manager can possibly prepare a grand design of these parts all at once. Design may have to be based on trial and error by setting up a pilot project. Evidence from the field could then be used to test whether a concept of service or a strategy for mobilisation of demand or any other component is appropriate to the environment.

Phasing cannot be tested through a pilot project. But most other components can be tested in pilot experiments. Important aids to strategy formulation are pilot experiments which are consciously planned to provide insights for evolving strategies for large national programmes. Launching pilot projects without deliberate plans and ignoring the process by which knowledge is transferred from experiments to the larger programmes are the weak points of some programmes. Those managing national programmes who did not work in pilot projects usually have difficulty understanding and integrating the lessons into their strategy. Sound strategies usually depend upon how pilot experimentation was planned and used as a learning device by programme managers. Pilot projects in national programmes are the counterparts of research and development projects in industrial enterprises.

5.4 Some guidelines for strategy formulation

Our discussion of SBS and DSR should not lead the reader to conclude that strategy formulation is a mechanical process. On the contrary, creating the building blocks and putting them together require imagination and a sound understanding of the environment. It is essentially an interactive process; those who are involved learn, adapt and resolve conflicts as they move on. While it is useful to know the components of a strategy, planning cannot be reduced to a series of simple steps. We will, therefore, pose a series of key questions to help designers and managers evolve programme strategies.

General questions

1. What are the operating goals of the programme?

2. Do they flow from the objectives given by the government?

3. Will the pursuit of multiple goals overburden the programme?

4. Have pilot projects been used to assist in programme design? How are they linked to the programme to maximise learning?

5. Has the achievement motivation (motivation to achieve

results, performance orientation) of the staff of the programme and the potential beneficiaries of the programme been considered in the formulation of the strategy?

6. What are the critical tasks indicated by the analysis of SBS and DSR?

Service-beneficiary-sequence

1. Does the programme call for a single service or multiple services?

2. If multiple, are they related or unrelated?

3. What is the degree of measurability of their inputs and outcomes

4. Do the services flow from the operating goal(s)?

5. Does the integration of inputs underlying the service(s) match beneficiary needs?

6. Are the service(s) consistent with the operating goal(s) and environmental complexity? If the technology is imported, how is its adaptation to local conditions ensured?

7. For whom are the service(s) meant?

8. Are the beneficiaries homogenous or diverse?

9. If multiple services are involved, are they meant for the same group of beneficiaries or diverse groups?

10. Is the combination of inputs designed to match the inability of the weaker section of beneficiaries to integrate inputs on their own?

11. If diverse beneficiary groups are involved, is it necessary to differentiate the service for them?

12. Is it advisable to extend the programme to the entire country all at once or should it be done in phases?

13. If phased implementation is better, what is the most useful basis for ensuring programme expansion?

Demand-supply-resource

1. Is there likely to be a demand problem for the programme?

2. What factors seem to inhibit demand?

3. What are the most appropriate interventions to help mobilise demand?

4. If demand appears to be a serious problem, what modifications are called for in the SBS components?

5. Is supply (service delivery) a more or less serious problem for the service than demand?

6. What specific interventions are called for to facilitate supply in terms of service design, logistics and delivery?

7. What strategic interventions are needed to ensure that strategies do not hamper the supply task?

8. Is it necessary to use private channels and sharing of costs with beneficiary groups (communities) to minimise the overload on the supply task?

9. Who are the key actors in the environment whose support needs to be mobilised in favour of the programme?

10. Who among them are influential on the demand side? Who will be influential on the supply side?

11. What specific resources or influences can be mobilised through these key actors?

12. What strategic interventions are needed to win the support of the key actors?

Each of these questions could be followed by sub-questions to probe each component further. This set of questions is by no means exhaustive. Rather it is a suggestive checklist which the designer or manager can adapt to his specific setting. The insights provided in this chapter could be used to add to this series of questions. These guidelines should be viewed as an aid to the creative process of designing a strategy consistent with the programme environment and not as a substitute for this very important process.

STRUCTURE: THE KEY DIMENSIONS   6

In chapter 3, we defined "structure", as the durable organisational arrangements by which a programme accomplishes its tasks. For example, programme tasks must be allocated among members of the organisation. Authority must be distributed to enable responsible managers and officials to perform their tasks. Reporting relationships and controls must be established to facilitate efficient task performance. Grouping activities, distributing authority to match the responsibility pattern in the organisation and clarifying the formal reporting relationships among those working in the organisation constitute the major elements of an organisational structure. Most of these issues are dealt with informally in small organisations, where the boss is in personal contact with all members and oversees all activities directly. But as organisations grow larger, no single person or group can manage all activities and people directly. It then becomes necessary to formalise relationships and create formal structures in which other managers and staff share responsibility and authority with the boss. This is not to deny the importance of informal structures and linkages in organisations.

Anyone familiar with small pilot projects and experiments will appreciate how personal involvement and supervision can accomplish common tasks. A formal organisational structure, delegation of powers and control systems seem alien to the needs of these small groups of committed workers. Nevertheless, when pilot projects are successful and are to be replicated on a larger scale by setting up a regional or national programme, the old, informal organisational arrangements seem to be unequal to the new tasks. Those brought up in the informal culture of the pilot projects may mourn the passing of a tradition, but there is no way to avoid a formalisation of the organisational structure and the growing shift to impersonal transactions.

Governments do recognise the importance of creating new organisational structures and reforming old ones, though they do not always act fast enough to deal with the problem. The creation of public sector organisations, for example, reflects the belief that the corporate form of organisation is more appropriate for manufacturing or commercial activities than the departmental form. Commissions and task forces are often set up by governments to recommend structural changes to fit the new task requirements. Ministries and departments are regrouped and sometimes abolished when a new government takes over. When strategies change, structures need to be realigned. In industrial enterprises, this is quite common. In fact, many cases have been reported of enterprises whose performance suffered when their structures failed to match their changed environments and strategies. Among the more successful enterprises are those who recognised this problem and realigned their strategies and structures.[1] Furthermore, some researchers have observed that the process of periodically realigning structures renews people's interest in their organisation and often helps them become more productive.

We will examine these dimensions of structure in this chapter. First of all, the manner in which tasks are divided (differentiated) into manageable components and then pulled together (integrated) is important. The structural form adopted by a programme reflects its approach to the differentiation and integration of activities. Second, a critical dimension of the structure is the degree to which it is centralised or decentralised. A third aspect concerns the extent of autonomy enjoyed by the programme organisation. The following sections will probe each of these dimensions.

6.1 Structural forms

Governments worldwide are characterised by hier-

---

[1] A. Chandler: Strategy and structure (Cambridge, Massachusetts, MIT Press, 1962).

archical structures which depend largely on the use of rules and authority to accomplish tasks. Each ministry or department which performs a set of tasks generally has a self-contained bureau or unit for each task. The staff of the bureau or unit perform the functions relevant to the task and report to a single boss who is responsible for the entire operation. There is a clearly defined line of authority which makes the structure hierarchical. Defence, public works, etc., are good examples of this functional structure. We use the term "functional" to mean that the sub-tasks are broken up according to the functions relevant to the service. It is the integration of these functions that the top administrator performs.

Since development programmes are normally initiated by ministries, the temptation is generally strong for the sponsor to prescribe for a programme its own structural form. And what is more, a functional structure often fits the needs of many programmes. Yet, when complex programmes whose tasks require different structures are launched, this standardised approach causes serious problems of performance. The appropriateness of a structure can be judged only in relation to a programme's strategy and environment. The designer should start with the goal, and tasks identified in the strategy and search for the best ways of differentiating and integrating the relevant activities and functions. When a programme (1) deals with a single service and (2) is relatively small, when (3) technology is simple and production processes are standardised, and when (4) the processing of information is relatively easy, it is possible that the functional, hierarchical structure will suffice.

Other structural forms are often better for complex development programmes. We discuss below three structural forms and the conditions under which they are better for a programme. Mixed forms and other adaptations of these structures are sometimes needed. Interested readers may consult the specialised writings on this subject.[1]

---

[1] P. Khandwalla: The design of organisations (New York, Harcourt-Brace, 1977); J. Galbraith: Organisation design (Reading, Massachusetts, Addison-Wesley, 1977) and H. Mintzberg: The structuring of organisations: A synthesis of the research (Englewood Cliffs, New Jersey, Prentice-Hall, 1979).

Functional structure

When an organisation deals with a single product or service, it can be managed by subdividing its activities into sets of complementary functions. To illustrate, in a dairy development programme four basic functions were identified. Providing services to farmers (extension, inputs) is one function; milk collection, quality control and transport another. Milk processing and marketing are the two remaining functions. There are several supporting functions too. Thus purchase of materials, finance, and manpower development can be treated as common services which facilitate the performance of the basic functions. Taken together, all these functions complement one another and each function has considerable uniformity in terms of its focus, skill requirements and internal communication. These functions are integrated at one place in the organisation, namely at the level of the chief executive, with the assistance of the heads of functional departments or units. The structure is functional in that the basic criterion for differentiating and integrating activities is the interdependence of functions.

When a programme grows larger geographically or adopts a multiple service strategy, a simple functional structure may no longer work. Many development programmes require much local adaptation of services. Remote control from distant headquarters by functional heads is often ineffective. Similarly, when a single service-oriented programme diversifies, the original set of functional groups may no longer be competent to supervise, support and control the additional services. For example, if an agricultural programme diversifies into health and education, its original functional departments will soon find themselves unequal to the task of managing the new services. Enterprises often adopt a product-based divisional structure when they diversify. For development programmes, this kind of divisional structure will probably be unsatisfactory. Matrix structures are increasingly used when programmes diversify their services or expand.

Figure 7 shows a typical functional structure, using an example taken from the Indian dairy programme agency.

Figure 7   Functional structure of a dairy programme agency

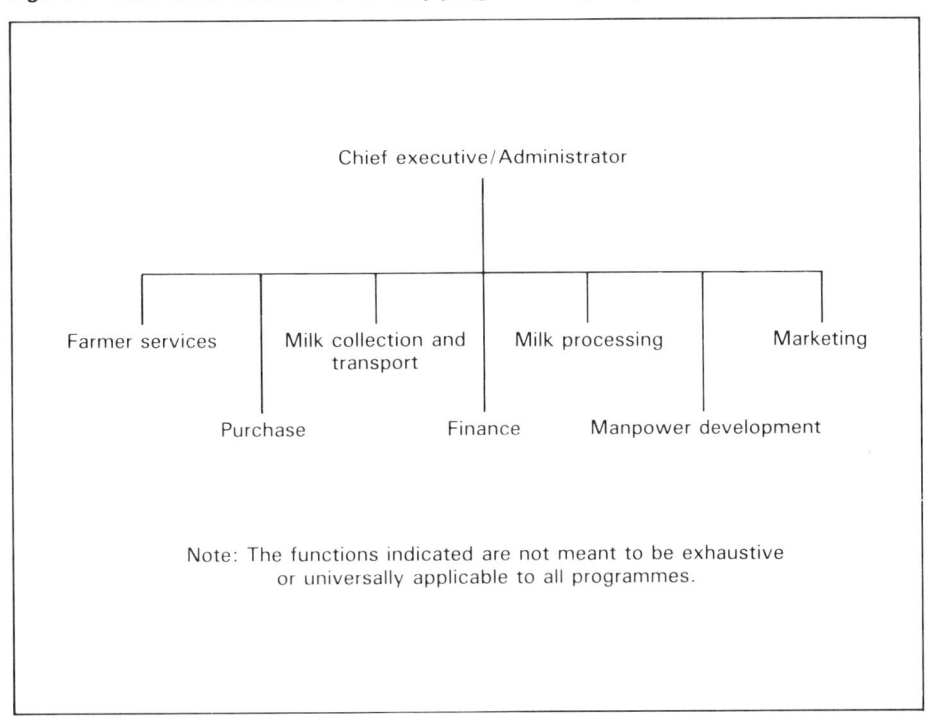

```
                    Chief executive/Administrator
        ┌───────────────┬──────────┬──────────────┐
   Farmer services   Milk collection   Milk processing   Marketing
                     and transport
            Purchase         Finance      Manpower development
```

Note: The functions indicated are not meant to be exhaustive or universally applicable to all programmes.

Matrix structure

The matrix form of organisation[1] operates under <u>dual authority</u>. In the functional structure, the line of control (hierarchy) is quite clear. In the matrix form, on the other hand, many members of staff have two bosses at the same time. For example, a single crop programme may be divided into several regions covering the entire country with a manager in charge of each region. The regional offices might have a complement of staff drawn from the different functional groups. These staff are members of two departments or groups simultaneously. They are responsible to the regional manager or administrator in the field as well as to the head of their respective functional departments for technical matters. Sometimes, these functional departments may be in the parent ministries, but the con-

---

[1] See, for example, K. Knight (ed.): <u>Matrix management: A cross-functional approach to management</u> (Farnborough, Hants, Gower Press, 1977).

Figure 8 Matrix structure of a dairy programme agency

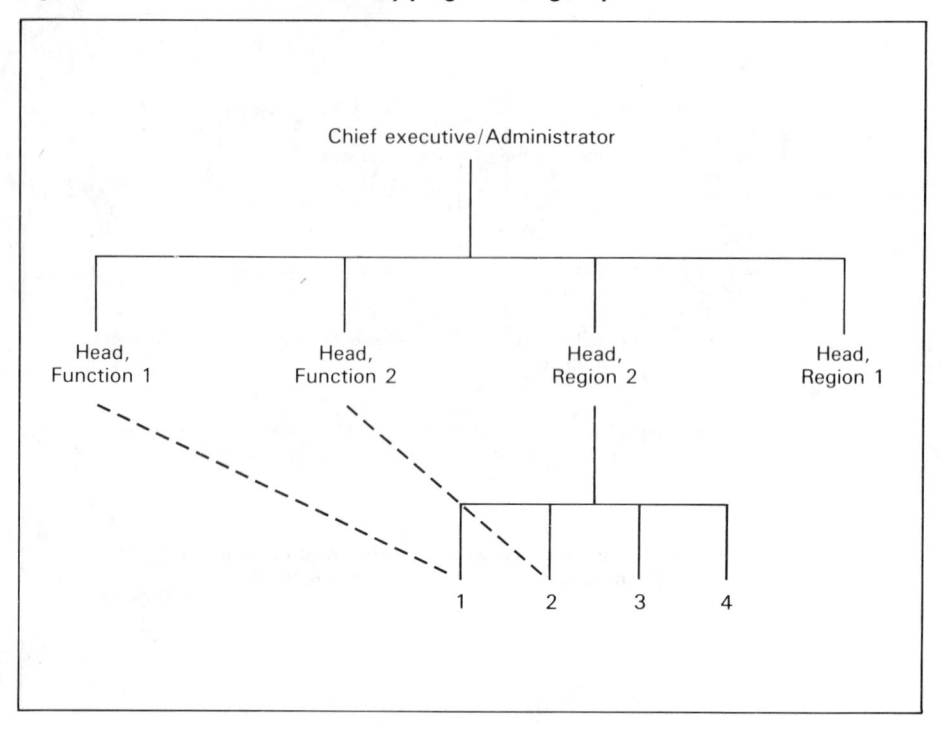

cept of dual membership and authority is still valid. This arrangement is common in multiple service programmes. Personnel for health and educational services in our earlier example may be drawn from the relevant ministries of government on the understanding that the technical back-up for the services will be provided by the latter. Thus the matrix form makes use of the principles of <u>specialisation</u> (functional) and <u>service</u> (substantive or spatial).

Figure 8 illustrates an organisation that is differentiated by both function and region. In Region 1, Managers 1 and 2 report to Head, Region 1, but are also controlled by the Heads of Functions 1 and 2 (the numbers are illustrative). The integrating role is now performed at lower levels (Managers 1 and 2) as well as at higher levels (regions and head office). The matrix form thus permits more decentralisation than does the functional form. There are usually more conflicts with this structure because more decisions are jointly made. But it is more appropriate when multiple regions or services are involved, and integration at lower levels and local adaptation are

Figure 9 Dual control

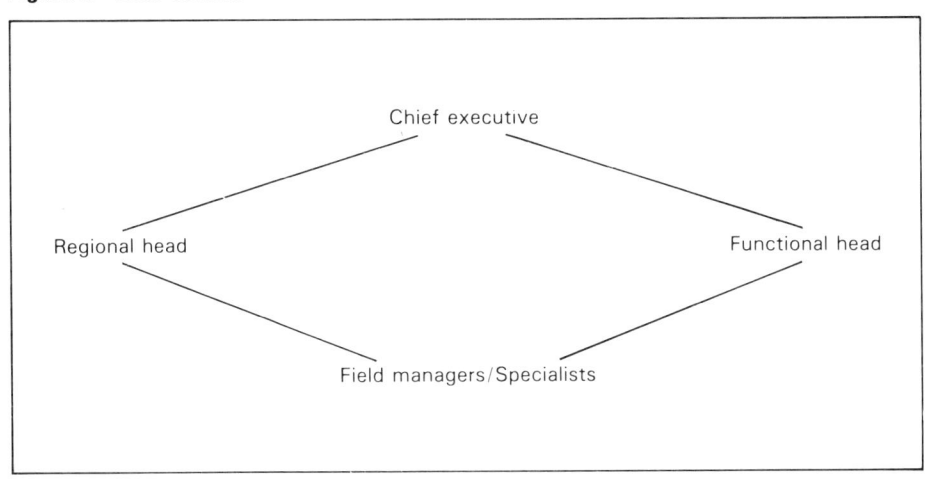

```
                    Chief executive
                    /            \
                   /              \
      Regional head                Functional head
                   \              /
                    \            /
                    Field managers/Specialists
```

desired because of increased environmental uncertainty, diversity and scope.

The managers working under the heads of Regions 1 and 2 in effect have two bosses. For operational matters, they are controlled by regional bosses. In technical or professional matters, they are controlled by their functional bosses. This dilemma of "dual control" is depicted in Figure 9. Dual authority is clearly a source of ambiguity and conflict in operating any programme. Managing the matrix structure calls for considerable sophistication, co-operative attitudes and willingness to negotiate when differences arise.

In a matrix structure, as a last resort, one tries to resolve conflicts at higher levels in the organisation. Dual authority merges into a unified command at the top. In large, complex development programmes, however, joint decisions and resolution of conflicts often require the formal co-operation of several organisations outside the programme agency. A structure that facilitates inter-organisational co-operation is more appropriate under these conditions than a functional or matrix form which assumes that a single organisation has full authority over all relevant decisions and actions.

Network structure

Few lead agencies can formally control other organisations or agencies whose participation is essential to a programme's success. To function effectively, the lead agency must often create a <u>network</u> of the relevant public and private agencies which it influences in different ways. The lead agency co-ordinates, but does not control. The network performs well only if the lead agency can influence its collaborators by joint allocation of funds, joint planning of activities, political support and review at higher levels.

The fact that an agency must use a network is evidence of its limited ability to control. A programme agency has different degrees of influence over the members of its network. It can exercise authority only over those who belong to its own organisation (e.g. field staff). Beneficiary groups, though dependent on the programme agency or other members of the network are not under its control. Accurate depictions of network structures become very complex because of the multiplicity of agencies and their varying degrees of influence.

Figure 10 illustrates the network structure of the Indonesian Population Programme. In this network, we can distinguish several types of influence involving the Population Board, the lead programme agency. First there was presidential <u>political support</u>, which was the single most important source of <u>influence</u> for the Board. The Board <u>directly controlled</u> only its own regional officers and field staff. Next, it <u>strongly influenced</u> co-operating ministries, such as health, education, religion and information. The Board had <u>strong influence</u> also over provincial governments which participated actively in the programme's implementation. Control over budgetary allocations to the participating agencies, joint planning and periodic review by the President were the means by which influence was exercised. The Board had no such direct influence over community organisations whose co-operation was essential to the programme's success. The Board had only a <u>weak influence</u> over these organisations. It used participation of the people and other motivating devices to elicit community co-operation.

In a population programme, several ministries (education, information, health, etc.) offer important inputs to the programme agency. State agencies may be critical to operational planning, implementation and local resolution

Figure 10 Network structure of the Indonesian population programme

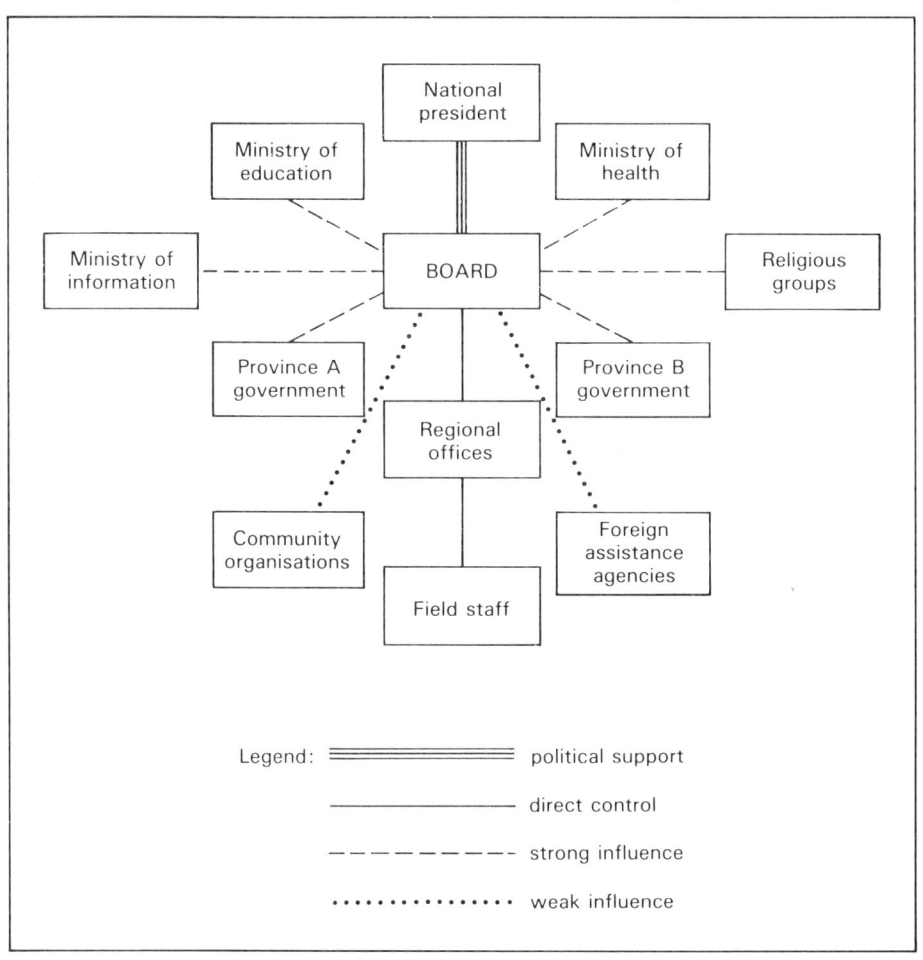

```
                        National
                        president
    Ministry of            ‖           Ministry of
    education              ‖            health
         \                 ‖              /
          \                ‖             /
Ministry of  ─ ─ ─ ─ ─   BOARD   ─ ─ ─ ─ ─  Religious
information                                  groups
          /      ⋮        │       ⋮    \
         /       ⋮        │       ⋮     \
    Province A   ⋮        │       ⋮   Province B
    government   ⋮     Regional   ⋮   government
                 ⋮     offices    ⋮
                 ⋮        │       ⋮
    Community    ⋮        │       ⋮    Foreign
    organisations         │            assistance
                          │            agencies
                       Field staff

Legend:  ══════════  political support
         ──────────  direct control
         ─ ─ ─ ─ ─   strong influence
         ·········   weak influence
```

of conflicts. Participation of community organisations may facilitate demand mobilisation and service delivery. Yet the programme agency does not control these organisations. If the programme agency can plan activities jointly with the other organisations and allocate funds to finance their part of the work (through a council, board, etc.) the network is likely to be more effective. In other words, the programme agency must have ways to influence the behaviour of other members of the network. Whether a programme will have a functional or matrix structure or move towards a network structure depends very much on its strategy and environment.

The Kenya Tea Development Authority, which organised almost all the inputs required by the tea farmers under its auspices (functional and vertical integration), performed well with a functional structure. Its use of network structure was quite limited. On the other hand, the Philippine Rice Programme, which depended on several agencies for diverse inputs and functions, depended heavily on the network structure. The National Food and Agriculture Council, which was responsible for this programme, co-ordinated the work of nearly 30 agencies, public and private, and provincial and local governments. Its sources of influences were joint planning, allocation of funds and mobilisation of demand through field staff and political support. Programme strategy and environment clearly had much to do with the structures that emerged in these cases. Structures seem to have followed strategies in both programmes.

6.2 Degree of decentralisation

Why decentralise, and how much? These questions are seldom asked by planners who design development programmes. Centralised structures, common in government ministries and departments, tend to be imposed on programmes. The differences between the structural requirements of the central systems of government and the field-oriented programme agencies are too often ignored.

On the other hand, some designers and researchers argue for decentralised structures for every programme without analysing its strategy or environment. They do not appreciate that the degree of decentralisation should vary depending on these factors. They do not weigh the gains of decentralisation against the costs of the increased complexity of management control and difficulty in finding the needed well-trained personnel at lower levels. Certainly, decentralisation increases the opportunities for participation by programme staff and beneficiaries. This is truely valuable by itself. Nevertheless, the barriers to decentralisation should be considered and ways of overcoming them planned for.

What conditions require decentralised structures? Generally, when the job requires flexible, quick decisions at the grass-roots level, centralised structures simply get overloaded and perform poorly. Four conditions call for greater decentralisation.

(1) When beneficiaries of the programme have diverse requirements, much local adaptation is called for. If there are different groups of farmers working under different climatic and soil conditions, the field staff will need to exercise considerable discretion to meet their divergent needs. Higher authorities cannot possibly make good rules for every situation or foresee and solve all problems.

(2) When demand for the service depends on speedy programme responses, decentralised structures perform better. Centralised structures invariably involve delays in decision making as issues move from one level to another. Delayed decisions and actions may fail to meet beneficiary needs. A popular example is the provision of credit to farmers. Referring their applications upwards and getting approvals from the top may take so long that by the time the money arrives, it is too late for the farmers to sow their crops. Farmers often then distrust the centralised structure and turn away from the programme.

(3) When vital information for decision making is generated only in consultation with the beneficiaries, decentralised structures often work best. Take nutrition programmes, for instance, where services are designed and delivery planned and organised centrally. Public response has been poor in most places, because these services were too standardised. Close contacts are needed with beneficiaries, whose concerns and preferences often change. The services should be designed in collaboration with communities using decentralised structures, because central authorities cannot analyse the necessary information or be sensitive to changing local conditions.

(4) When responsible participation of field staff and beneficiaries in programme planning and implementation is conducive to good performance, decentralised structures often work best. Social programmes, which do not offer direct and immediate economic gains to beneficiaries, work best when beneficiaries participate in programme planning and implementation to motivate them to respond to the programme. This logic applies as well to field staff. Those who enjoy some local autonomy and feel that they can

influence decisions and actions are likely to work more enthusiastically for the programme. This happened in the Indonesian Population Programme; village communities actively participated in its work and the field staff took greater initiative in adapting their services locally.

How decentralised a structure should be can be decided only with reference to each situation. Three principles should be considered, however. *First*, decentralisation does not mean that all functions are decentralised. Even in a decentralised structure, some functions are centralised. For example, functions involving considerable economies of scale and highly specialised knowledge may remain centralised. Bulk purchases, certain research and development activities and allocation of funds are often better organised centrally, whereas operational planning, detailed service designs and service delivery may be decentralised. *Second*, the four conditions discussed above also indicate the kinds of functions which need to be decentralised. Broadly speaking, those functions which facilitate local adaptation of services, reduce the overload on central information processing, stimulate demand for services, and strengthen participation should be decentralised. *Third*, the degree of decentralisation should be determined in conjunction with the programme agency's ability to develop enough skilled managers to manage the decentralised structure. When there are practical problems in influencing the new structure, care should be taken to move cautiously and, if necessary, in phases.

In summary, the choice of a structural form does not necessarily imply a precise degree of decentralisation or centralisation. Functional structures can be centralised or decentralised. Matrix and network structures are generally more decentralised than centralised. But which functions should be centralised and which decentralised can be determined only by considering the criteria discussed above.

6.3 *Organisational autonomy*

Some programme organisations enjoy more autonomy than others do. By autonomy, we mean the degree of independence from the parent ministry in important areas of decision making and action. For example, a programme agency that does not need its parent ministry's approval for internal allocation of funds, appointment and promotion of its personnel, operational plans and related decisions enjoys a high degree of autonomy in these critical areas. Complete autonomy is an unrealistic expectation for programmes sponsored and funded by government. The latter is bound to exercise some control over all its programmes. Ideally, governments should exercise <u>strategic control</u> over their programmes and leave <u>operational decisions</u> to the programme leaders. Thus approval of the programme budget, top level appointments and review of performance are aspects of strategic control. Autonomy gets eroded when government officials interfere too often in the programme's operational decisions. When hesitant programme managers refer operational decisions back to the ministry, it is difficult to avoid delays and a dilution of accountability. When the government grants some organisational autonomy to a programme, it should also have the will and ability to monitor its performance and hold its management accountable for agreed-upon results or outcomes. But no public programme can be completely autonomous.

The degree of organisational autonomy is usually clarified when defining a programme's structure. The legal form of organisation created for the programme yields important clues about its autonomy. For example, when a corporate form is given to a programme agency, there are likely to be legal provisions to ensure it some measure of autonomy. Agencies organised as part of the ministry or department usually enjoy less autonomy. Legal structures are important insofar as they formally define the extent to which an organisation can depart from the norms and practices of its parent. We shall refer to this as <u>nominal</u> autonomy. However, <u>the effective autonomy</u> an organisation enjoys may well exceed or fall below what is permitted legally. Organisations in both public and private sectors earn some autonomy from their sponsors or supervising authorities. Thus, the trust and support of political leaders or top administrators in government may bestow on a programme agency a degree of <u>effective autonomy</u> that exceeds its <u>nominal autonomy</u>. We shall call the difference between the two <u>induced autonomy</u>. Induced or earned autonomy occurs because those who have authority can also use discretion to augment a programme's effective autonomy. It is, of course, true that programme managers often do not use all the effective autonomy they have.

A programme's strategy and the complexity of its environment yield clues about the degree of organisational autonomy it requires. In designing a programme's organisational structure, one should ensure that it has enough autonomy. For instance, a programme that operates in an uncertain environment needs more effective autonomy than a programme in a stable environment.

The Indian Dairy Programme agency, the National Dairy Development Board, was set up as a semi-autonomous public agency and not as an integral part of the Ministry of Agriculture. Apart from the legal (nominal) autonomy given to it, the Board induced additional autonomy through some innovative changes in its sources of funding. Its good performance no doubt persuaded the Ministry to grant it a degree of effective autonomy far in excess of its original nominal autonomy. For a programme which had to deal with sensitive milk markets and thousands of small farmers whose response could be volatile, a high degree of autonomy was essential.

An effective way to stretch limited organisational autonomy is to involve relevant voluntary and private organisations and local communities. Some parts of the programme's activities could be efficiently performed by such agencies. Some activities might be subcontracted to private firms and small entrepreneurs. The rigidities of government systems will not apply to them and hence they will be able to deliver the goods faster and cheaper. In the Philippine Rice Programme, for example, private rural banks provided credit to farmers and private companies distributed pesticides and other inputs. Thus the programme agency responded to farmers with greater flexibility. In population programmes, voluntary family planning agencies often perform certain functions with considerable flexibility. Thus, it is possible for a programme to enhance its effective autonomy by letting private or voluntary organisations perform some tasks which they can do more efficiently.

We have discussed in this chapter three important dimensions of the organisational structure. We have argued that structural choices are neither self-evident nor uniform. Structure must be adapted to the programme environment and strategy. In the public context, there are limits to the flexibility a programme may enjoy in altering its structure. A government may be unwilling to try out a new organisational form, decentralise programme management or grant adequate autonomy. If so, there is a case for limiting the strategy of the programme and aligning it to what is feasible in terms of structural changes. There should be a mutual adaptation between stra- tegy and structure. A "fit" between the two is essential. When the two do not match, performance will suffer. Se- cond, when environmental conditions and strategy change, structure must be realigned to fit the change. Part of the top management's function is to be sensitive to these changes and to take steps to realign the programme strategy and structure.

6.4 Some guidelines for structural choices

First, one must analyse the critical features of a programme's environment and strategy. The choice of the structural form, degree of decentralisation and autonomy can be derived from such an analysis. The questions posed below should be followed up by a detailed analysis.

Environment and strategy

1. How large is the programme? Is its size and geographical spread such that control through hierarchical authority will be feasible?

2. How diverse are the beneficiaries? Do they have significantly different needs and problems which necessitate a differentiation of the programme's service(s)?

3. Can the inputs for the programme service be organised within the purview of the programme agency? If not, will it have to depend on the active collaboration of a variety of agencies to obtain and integrate the needed inputs?

Structural forms

1. What is the best way of differentiating the tasks or activities of the programme (by function, service, region, or a combination)?

2. What are the best integrative mechanisms which can be derived to pull together the subdivided tasks?

3. If the programme must make use of the matrix form, what steps should be taken to ensure that dual authority will be accepted in the organisation?

4. If a network structure is adopted, what sources of influence are available to the programme agency to make it work?

5. What role can the programme offer non-governmental agencies (private, co-operative and beneficiary groups) in the network for the planning and delivery of services?

6. Does the nature of the strategy require that the structure be placed outside the purview of any single ministry? If so, who in government should be responsible for the programme?

Decentralisation

1. Does the diversity among beneficiaries call for considerable local adaptation of the programme service?

2. Does response to the needs of beneficiaries require speedy decisions and actions at the local level?

3. Does the design of the service have to be made in con- sultation with beneficiaries at the grass roots level?

4. Is participation by staff and beneficiaries in planning and implementation likely to contribute to improved programme performance?

5. If answers to the above questions indicate the need for a decentralised structure, what are the specific functions to be decentralised? Why?

6. Which functions should be centralised? Why (economies of scale, specialised knowledge)?

7. Assuming that decentralisation is desirable, will the programme have enough trained manpower to manage a

decentralised structure? If not, can the structural change be phased over time?

8. Do the gains of decentralisation outweigh its costs?

Autonomy

1. Will programme performance be hurt if departures from government norms, practices and decision making process are not feasible?

2. In which areas of management are such departures most critical (financial, personnel, policy making, etc.)? Why?

3. How far can legal autonomy provide the needed flexibility?

4. If there are limits to legal autonomy, are there ways of inducing or earning additional autonomy?

5. What measures of performance (outcomes, services, efficiency indices) can be provided to the government to facilitate its monitoring and review functions?

6. If adequate autonomy cannot be obtained, what can be done to minimise performance problems by assigning additional responsibilities in the structure to beneficiaries and non-governmental groups in the planning, implementation and resource generation of the programme?

PROCESS INTERVENTIONS 7

In chapter 3, we defined organisational processes as the instruments by which managers influence the behaviour of the employees and beneficiaries of a development programme. Business enterprises are well known for the ways they motivate their staff, for example through financial incentives linked to individual or group performance. Their ability to make decisions quickly shows how flexible their internal processes are. In contrast, it is often said that governmental processes are rigid. Slow decision making and the failure of internal procedures to motivate staff are often given as limitations of governmental organisational processes. These organisational processes are concerned with "how" decisions are made and how actions are taken. Strategy, on the other hand, focuses on the "content" or "what" of the decisions. Understanding the internal processes of a programme tells us much about its problems of implementation.

7.1 Governmental processes

Since governments initiate and control development programmes, governmental processes are regularly transferred to programmes. Uncritical adoption of these processes is a major problem of many programmes. Thus, we must first examine the basic features of governmental processes. First, governmental processes of decision making and implementation are heavily dominated by hierarchical authority, especially in ministries and departments which are part of the executive branch of the government. While the legislative branch may well follow participative and democratic processes, executive departments operate as if only those in authority have the right and proper knowledge of what needs to be done. The subordinates must carry out their instructions or orders. In formulating a programme strategy, allocating funds and choosing a structure, heads of ministries or departments commonly convey their decisions to subordinates for implementation. Centralised government structures reinforce this practice. Those below in the hierarchy have little discretion in this "top-down" process of decision making.

Second, governmental processes generally focus on observing procedures rather than on achieving results. Monitoring and control processes are designed to ensure that expenditures are incurred in accordance with government rules and regulations with scant attention to the purposes achieved or services generated. Procedures for selecting personnel focus on whether the norms and practices of government have been adhered to rather than whether candidates are suitable for their jobs. This may have worked reasonably when governments were solely concerned with maintaining law and order, the outputs of which were difficult to define or measure.

Third, the processes of government are less flexible than those of the private sector. When tasks and programmes change, governments adapt their processes slowly and with great difficulty. Consequently, processes become standardised and routinised, and "precedents" determine the course of decision and action. To illustrate, central decision making often prescribes a standard design for a programme in diverse regions of the country. The recruitment process may be kept inflexible despite the differing requirements of programmes. Equity and justice, rather than results, dominate the choices. Modifying internal processes to suit the situation are seen as improper and discriminatory by those affected by the decisions and actions. Here again, where law and order decisions and revenue collection alone are involved, purely equity-oriented processes have considerable merit. But when conditions and tasks change, and the results of programmes are adversely affected by standardised and inflexible processes, their rationale deserves a fresh examination. Most of these processes and their inbuilt inflexibility arose from traditional government functions carried out by central systems. Development programmes are seldom concerned with these functions. Nor can they be operated as part of the central systems of government. They are often field-oriented activities which succeed only when adapted to varying local conditions. Political and bureaucratic leaders in LDCs must appreciate these important differences and encourage programmes to adopt internal processes consistent with their goals and environments.

Four critical organisational processes which must be adapted for development programmes to succeed are (1) participation, (2) human resource development, (3) monitoring and control and (4) motivation. Several other processes, such as budgeting and performance evaluation, are also at work, but these four capture the essence of decision making and action in most programmes.

7.2 The participation process

In many poor countries, it is not uncommon for facilities and services to be created and offered to people, who then fail to use them satisfactorily. Many drinking water supply schemes have been set up, but the women, the traditional water-carriers, do not use the costly pumps installed by the programme agency. Rural housing is often built which people refuse to live in. Many factors may be responsible for these failures, yet fundamentally the facilities were not designed for the special needs and problems of the intended beneficiaries. This happens when decision making processes exclude the participation of those affected because decision makers assume that people need certain basic facilities. They focus too soon on the technology and economics of the services, ignoring the match between perceptions of beneficiaries and the services and facilities offered.

Contrast this with the Japanese practice of extensive consultation with all concerned when reaching important decisions on key issues. This process of building a consensus consumes much time, but once the consensus is reached, implementation is fast and efficient. What appears to be tedious and cumbersome in making choices turns out to be effective in achieving results.

Thus, participative decision making processes are often more effective because they bring about a better "fit" between what beneficiaries want and what the programmes provide. <u>Participation facilitates implementation</u> because the motivation to build and use the services will be stronger when the participants have agreed upon the course of action. Participative processes improve <u>knowledge</u> about the programme service and strengthen <u>commitment</u> to implementation by the programme staff and beneficiaries.

Participation as a goal

Participation is not only a way to improve programme performance but also a goal in itself. Many argue that participation should be encouraged because it is essential to human development and self-reliance. All development activities, it is argued, must mobilise people's active participation. Only then will they learn to do things for themselves and stand on their own feet. Poor countries often tend to encourage and perpetuate dependency and subservience through authoritarian government structures and decision processes. Participation is an antidote for this and an essential step towards helping people to develop themselves. It contributes to their improvement.

Participation can be encouraged in many ways. Individuals can play decisive roles in key decisions affecting them. Democratic elections are good examples of this process in politics. Members of co-operatives which organise economic activities also play a similar role. In development programmes, groups of beneficiaries can be involved directly in planning and implementation, and sometimes they are represented through local organisations or traditional local structures which have specific responsibilities within the programmes. Several studies show that programme outcomes are more successful where local organisations actively participate.[1]

Economic programmes which offer substantial economic incentives to beneficiaries and whose services are largely standardised can succeed with little participation by beneficiaries and field staff in decision making. Social programmes with weak economic incentives and many local adaptations need much participation. Of course, some participation is needed in economic programmes, but the degree of participation and its relative importance varies. Why is this so?

---

[1] See Uphoff and Esman: <u>Local organisation for rural development: analysis of Asian experience</u>, RDC Monograph No. 19 (Ithaca, NY, Cornell University Press, 1974).

Consider the Rice Development Programme of the Philippines. When rice farmers found that the new programme would give them much higher outputs, guaranteed prices and high incomes, they willingly followed the advice and instructions of the field staff. Individual incentives were strong and individual action was adequate to increase rice output. The fact that farmers did not formally participate in planning the programme or its implementation did not reduce their response to it. Contrast this with the Indonesian Population Programme. Its early attempt to manage the programme through a "top down" process soon ran into serious problems; the response from the rural public began to taper off. When villagers were encouraged to participate in the planning and implementation of the programme, public response increased. This social programme did not offer people immediate economic returns. Instead it called for changes of attitudes and behaviour by people who were influenced by strong social customs and values. Their response could be changed only through their own communities and leaders active in the change process. In this case, participation created commitment towards the programme in the communities and a willingness to generate and share resources. The field staff also contributed more effectively to the programme as they felt that they had greater internal autonomy and a larger role than in other more hierarchically controlled programmes. Working with rural communities in different parts of a country with considerable diversity called for responsiveness to local problems and the ability to adapt the service to local conditions. The decentralised structure of the programme and its participative process enabled the staff to do this effectively.

Why don't governments encourage the participative process more? Generally, for three reasons:

(1) The belief that only those in authority have the knowledge to plan and act discourages participation. Countries with strong civil services steeped in traditional styles of administration find it difficult to decentralise and share decision making with others. Specialists and scientists who have joined the bureaucracy strengthen this belief. They believe that they have the requisite knowledge and that others need only follow their instructions.

(2) The view that response or action in the field can be enforced through the use of authority is also deeply entrenched in government. Few recognise that response to many programmes must be generated through persuasion, mobilisation of demand and proper incentives. That participation is a powerful way to generate commitment and response is too rarely appreciated.

(3) Those in authority hesitate to decentralise and let others participate in decision making and action for fear that the latter would make mistakes. No doubt, field staff and beneficiaries will err. However, those at the top also often make mistakes, especially when they lack the necessary information and have neither the skills nor the time to adapt programme services to diverse environments. Top administrators too seldom appreciate that beneficiaries and implementing staff are engaged in a process of learning and that mistakes can be minimised only by letting them learn by doing.

Role of non-governmental organisations (NGOs)

Though many development programmes call for a greater degree of beneficiary participation, beneficiaries are seldom sufficiently organised to participate in decision making and implementation. This happens when they are too poor and lack organisational and leadership skills. The programme leadership, working under the governmental constraints, is often unable to perform its mobilising role. When this occurs, it is appropriate to invite NGOs (also known as voluntary agencies) to help mobilise the beneficiaries. NGOs are generally more familiar with local people and conditions and are more flexible in their internal decision making processes and structures. They may also be more effective in encouraging the beneficiaries to participate in and respond to the programme.

> The adult education programme in India is a national programme of the government where local voluntary agencies (NGOs) were responsible for local planning and implementation. In earlier years, when the government directly managed the programme exclusively through its civil service, progress was unsatisfactory. NGOs distinctly improved the programme performance because they could make participative processes work locally. Similarly, in Mexico, a rural education

programme was successfully organised through the active participation of village communities and their committees which supervised the working of their rural schools.

Thus governments should very actively seek the cooperation and support of NGOs and other local groups in managing development programmes which need much beneficiary participation and mobilisation, especially if the bureaucratic machinery cannot cope with this challenge.

7.3 Human resource development processes

Two components of this process need to be discussed separately. First, the human resources for a programme must be identified and brought on board. This is "selection". Second, they must be equipped and oriented suitably for their jobs in changing environments. This is their "development" process. Both aspects must be organised simultaneously.

Staff selection

Inflexible, and sometimes unsuitable, government selection processes are common in many development programmes. Governments rarely grant autonomy to their programme managers in selecting staff. Consequently, programmes are unable to find the people who can perform their developmental tasks. However, most successful programmes were allowed considerable flexibility in personnel selection.

Programmes which need diverse skills will require broad, open sources of recruitment. The practice of using "seconded" staff from the parent ministry runs counter to this. Multiple sources of talent must be searched to attract different skills. Competent staff are not rare in government, but processes designed to attract staff only from government severely constrains a programme's search for the right talent. For example, those who worked on a pilot project and produced good results are often best equipped to manage a national programme. The selection process should emphasise the search for the right people for the tasks rather than to explicitly or implicitly limit the sources of personnel.

In the Philippine Rice Programme, while extension staff were drawn from the Agricultural Ministry, special care was taken to give key roles to the extension technicians who had successfully worked and gained valuable experience in the pilot project. The latter were deliberately assigned to train the newly recruited staff of the programme. In the Indian Dairy Programme, deputationists from government departments were seldom recruited. Most staff were drawn from institutions relevant to the programme. The most important of these was the "Amul Dairy", a highly successful farmer co-operative which was the model adopted by the new dairy programme. Flexibility in selection was an important feature of the autonomy enjoyed by the Indian Dairy Board.

Staff development

Selection and training are key processes available to programme managers to match their staff to tasks. Many programmes fail because no effort was made to prepare the staff to perform their tasks. Even where staff have been carefully selected, they usually need to be trained and developed to fit the roles planned for them in the programme. Further, training is not a one-shot affair, but a continuing activity, because staff need to be upgraded and re-oriented to the changing requirements and challenges facing the programme. Top management's duty is to attach priority to staff development processes and to ensure that it operates effectively.

Three aspects of staff development deserve mention.

(1) That training can create appropriate skills and attitudes is generally understood. Many governments, however, are reluctant to train people away from their jobs. While much can be learned on the job, development programmes invariably call for skills, understanding of new approaches and different ways of dealing with beneficiaries. A systematic understanding of these skills and attitudes require both specially-organised training as well as on-the-job experience. One is not a substitute for the other; they complement and reinforce each other.

(2) Training can aid development of commitment, which is an important motivator for those working in programmes.

The staff development process can be used not only to impart skills, but also to create a sense of belonging among the people, pride in their work and a belief that they are engaged in important nation-building tasks. Programmes are seldom able to offer monetary rewards in proportion to the results achieved by the staff. But by strengthening their identification with the cause of the programme, their motivation to perform is strengthened. Thus successful programmes create meaning in people's lives.

(3) The development and training process should focus on both the staff and beneficiaries of the programme. They are partners in a common endeavour. Beneficiaries, when properly oriented and trained, can make the tasks of the staff much lighter. Yet, this is an aspect of human resource development which seldom receives attention. Certainly, organising client training and orientation is more difficult than staff training. The former are not within the programme manager's control, nor are they likely to be a homogenous and pre-selected lot.

Studies of several successful programmes testify to the power of training. In the Mexican Rural Education Programme, training of the young instructors for imparting skills and to create commitment played an important role. In fact, at the end of their training, candidates who did not measure up to the challenge ahead were weeded out. Training thus aided selection. In the Kenyan Tea Development Authority, farmers as well as the field staff were trained. The Authority had its own training schools. In the Indian Dairy Programme, farmers from different parts of the country were brought to Amul Dairy as part of an orientation programme. The Philippine Rice Programme invested heavily in the training of its field staff and also organised training for farmers in different regions. In fact, a common feature of the successful programmes is the high priority they attach to the human resource development process. The match between the people and their tasks was achieved through the conscious use of this important process.

7.4 The monitoring and control process

The monitoring and control processes of governments

in developing countries reflect their interest in the observance of procedures and rules rather than in the achievement of results. Those who monitor and control programmes are concerned about how money was spent and whether the proper procedures were followed. Violation of procedures and norms in vogue attracts censure from those in authority. Lack of performance, on the other hand, rarely invites penalties. Of course, procedures are important. However, the processes of successful programmes focus more on performance and outcomes than solely on procedures and operational decisions.

Development programmes are field-oriented activities whose beneficiaries and field staff are often scattered over vast areas. Personal supervision and monitoring by the leadership are difficult. As programmes and their environments become increasingly complex, monitoring and control must become more systematic, but not too complex for field staff to respond to and understand. Monitoring systems should be simple, compact and yet sophisticated in design. Is this a contradiction in terms?

Simplicity and sophistication

Systems can be simple, compact and sophisticated at the same time. A system that can be organised and managed by the people who furnish the data and those who use the data is simple. Monitoring often fails when the data requested are too voluminous and complex for those who have to supply them. If data requirements are not understood or cannot be easily assembled by the field staff, their response is unlikely to be helpful. A _compact_ system implies brevity and precision. Field staff are busy and often short of resources; their time is best utilised when the information to be sought is precise and brief. Vague questions attract vague replies. Inadequately explained information requirements tend to be intepreted and defined in diverse ways. Being precise, clear and brief in seeking information therefore has considerable merit. Brief, simple information systems need considerable _sophistication in design_. Designing a one-page reporting format is more difficult than preparing a ten-page one. The choice of data and their inter-relationships must be carefully weighed. It takes time and thought to design simple, sophisticated systems that characterise successful development programmes.

Critical dimensions: what and how

The monitoring process can help programme managers only when the information reported is of direct interest to top management, when they realise what information top management uses and how it is used. First, information gathered should be of direct interest to top management. When the top managers seek and use information, it gives strong signals to other members of the organisation. They, in turn, take monitoring more seriously when they realise that information is used. The question of who is concerned about information is significant because it conveys to others the nature of information being sought. For example, when programme managers monitor results and the progress of the key tasks assigned to their staff, the latter pay more attention to these aspects. On the other hand, when the focus is on the observance of procedures and rules rather than on the achievement of goals, the staff will concentrate on adherence to procedures and ignore goal-oriented performance. Thus what information is sought makes a difference. Third, how the information is used also matters. When monitoring is not systematic and feedback is not regularly given to those whose operations are being monitored, the motivation of the latter will be adversely affected. When programme managers fail to analyse the information furnished to them or do not utilise the findings to take appropriate action, those who work with them are unlikely to take monitoring seriously. Generally speaking, information and analysis of a post mortem type, which do not feed back into the decision making channels of the programme agency, will not be seen as useful by operating staff. Post-mortem evaluation has its place, but should be distinguished from managerial evaluation and feedback which is crucial for improving the performance of ongoing programmes.

The monitoring process works both formally and informally. For development programmes which operate in difficult environments, field visits by supervisors for informal gathering and sharing of information are as important as formal information systems. A difficult environment is one with limited communication facilities, and beneficiaries and field staff whose skills and sophistication in operating formal systems are limited. Personal discussions and surveys often generates more useful insights and understanding than formal reports. As a programme expands and increases in scope, programme managers may have to depend more on formal monitoring.

Many successful programmes bear eloquent testimony to the importance of the monitoring process. In the Indian Dairy Development Programme, a monthly report from the district union dairy forms the corner-stone of the formal monitoring process. It is a one-page report which seeks information on milk procurement, prices, content, progress on farmer organisations, services to farmer members, milk processing and sales revenue. The design is simple, yet extremely sophisticated and provides detailed instructions to the respondents on how to prepare the report. In addition, the Dairy Board also gathers regular information on the urban dairies and the new plants being set up. The Indian Programme gets regular reports on the functioning of the village co-operatives through the reports submitted by supervisors who visit the field. Their reports not only highlight the progress of individual societies, but also the problems identified by them in the field. This is an example of using informal sources of information, without loading the local staff with heavy reporting work. Though the information system appears to be simple, it is efficient, timely and fast in terms of the feedback given to the constituents of the programme.

7.5 The motivation process

We have already mentioned some relationships among human resource development, monitoring and motivation of programme staff. Motivation is complex and is affected by more than staff development and monitoring. Traditional government bureaucracies have often believed in the power of authority to motivate people to get things done. Once orders are given from above, it is believed that those below would implement them. It is too rarely recognised that different motivators are often at work in different activities. In economic activities, for example, economic incentives are often the key motivators. In many organisations, other motivators such as status and recognition, participation and autonomy, and ideological commitment are significant. There is thus a mix of incentives and factors which motivate the participants in a development programme.

Nature of the programme

No standard motivation process or mix of incentives is best for all types of development programmes. The nature of the programme and its environment generally indicate which incentives are likely to work. The incentives that work for the programme staff are seldom appropriate for programme beneficiaries. Most developing countries have found that the use of authority is a very poor motivator in development programmes. Authority is more useful in regulatory than in development programmes. In socio-economic development, one must persuade and win people's hearts and minds to new ideas, practices and behaviour so that they eventually perceive these to be in their own interest. Programmes which carry out economic tasks (agriculture, industry, etc.) can use economic incentives effectively, as long as a distinction is made between motivators for staff and motivators for programme beneficiaries. Economic programmes which do not make these distinctions often perform poorly.

Social programmes which do not offer direct economic gains to the beneficiaries can use few economic incentives. Programmes in literacy, preventive health care, family planning, etc., focus on social change. Their staff need adequate monetary rewards which can seldom be linked directly to staff performance. Recognition of good work, creation of commitment, and a sense of internal autonomy to plan one's own work is likely to elicit healthy responses from the staff. Beneficiaries of such programmes are motivated better through participation in planning and implementation. Competition between communities and community pride are often excellent motivators. Individual incentives to motivate beneficiaries are usually counter-productive in programmes which require co-operation among members of the community and staff. Thus, one must carefully consider the nature of the programme and its strategy when determining the mix of incentives for motivating the staff and beneficiaries. One must also often separate the motivational needs of the staff from those of beneficiaries as well as distinguishing between the motivators available to economic and social programmes.

Successful agricultural development programmes almost always have stable, adequate procurement prices as part of their strategy to motivate farmers to respond to their services. Farmers generally ignore programmes with inadequate or fluctuating "farm gate" prices. The Kenyan Tea Programme and the Indian Dairy Programme consider this to be an important incentive motivating their members. Economic incentives for staff also played a moderate role in the Kenyan Programme and the Philippines Rice Programme. In the Kenyan Programme, most staff came from the Ministry of Agriculture and received about 10 per cent more money than at the Ministry. Those who did not perform well were not fired, but were sent back to the Ministry. On the other hand, social programmes such as the Chinese Public Health Programme do not show any evidence of motivating their staff and beneficiaries through the use of economic incentives. Their behaviour was influenced more through the use of commitment creation, participation and local autonomy. In fact, the Indonesian Programme discontinued the use of economic incentives to individual field workers when it was found to be counter-productive.

In general, development programmes seldom have much flexibility in rewarding their staff monetarily in line with their performance. This is in contrast to industrial enterprises which rely largely on economic incentives and disincentives. Programme managers should therefore be innovative in using indirect rewards for their staff. For example, good performance should be taken into account when promotions are considered. Opportunities for self-development should be available to those who perform well. Accelerated increments can sometimes be offered to deserving personnel. Thus there are ways of providing economic rewards indirectly even where elaborate schemes linking performance to economic incentives cannot be put into effect. Such approaches, reinforced by non-economic incentives such as recognition of work and enlarged work roles suitably adapted to the programme setting, can often motivate those staff who can be motivated.

7.6 Some guidelines for programme managers

The questions below can help programme managers become aware of their choices and options when designing the internal processes of their organisations. Using the insights offered in this chapter, additional questions may be asked and answered in light of the specific contents of each programme.

Participation

1. Does the parent ministry or programme manager have the knowledge necessary to design and implement the programme? If not, can the participative process be used to improve the strategy and implementation of the programme?

2. Does the programme service have to be adapted to suit diverse local conditions? What are its implications for participation?

3. Does public response to the programme call for considerable participation by beneficiaries?

4. Is it important to generate local resources to support the programme?

5. Is the creation and strengthening of self-reliance an important goal of the programme?

Human resource development

1. How diverse are the skills and talents needed by the programmes? Can they be found within the government bureaucracy?

2. What are the potential sources of staff recruitment?

3. How much autonomy does the programme need to evolve its own selection process?

4. Are pilot projects available as a source for the selection and development of staff?

5. Is the training process designed to match the people to their tasks?

6. Is training used only for acquiring skills, or also for creating commitment among staff?

7. Does the process contribute to the development of beneficiaries?

Monitoring and control

1. Does the process focus on goals and results or on

procedures and operating decisions?

2. How well is the information system designed to fit the limitations of the programme environment?

3. Are the programme leaders committed to the monitoring and use of information to improve performance?

4. Does the monitoring process provide fast feedback to those who have to take corrective action?

5. How frequent and regular is the feedback to the field?

6. Is the programme geared to using informal sources of information in addition to the formal sources?

7. Does the reporting system impose an undue burden on the field staff?

Motivation

1. Do the monitoring and development processes postively motivate the staff and beneficiaries of the programme?

2. Is the mix of economic and non-economic incentives designed to motivate the staff and beneficiaries?

3. Does the motivation process distinguish between the needs of staff and beneficiaries?

4. Do the programme leaders have the flexibility to adapt its mix of incentives to the changing needs of the programme?

5. Does the mix of incentives support the strategy and structure of the programme? If not, how should the motivation process be adapted to play a reinforcing role?

ORCHESTRATION OF CONGRUENCE   8

In chapter 3, we mentioned that the factors examined in detail so far work together to produce a "synergistic" effect on programme performance. While each factor alone is important, when there is "congruence" among them the programmes perform better. Agricultural production was used to show that only the proper combination of inputs (seeds, water, fertiliser, etc.) yields the most output. Higher output is not merely due to the contribution of the individual inputs, but more importantly due to the power of a specific combination of inputs when matched to the specific conditions of the crop, its soil, etc. The term "congruence" describes this combination. Any reduction in one input relative to others reduces output significantly.

In a development programme, interrelationships among its environment, strategy, structure and processes are similar to the organic relationships among the inputs of a crop. Having discussed these four factors in detail, we can now depict strategic management more completely in figure 11 than we did in figure 4.

Figure 11 shows how congruence is achieved by adapting the strategy, structure and processes of a programme to its environment. Environment is the least influenceable of these. The programme leaders and the government can manipulate the other three within limits. When they are congruent, their interaction creates synergy which cannot be explained by any one factor alone.

109

Figure 11 The four factors: linkages and performance

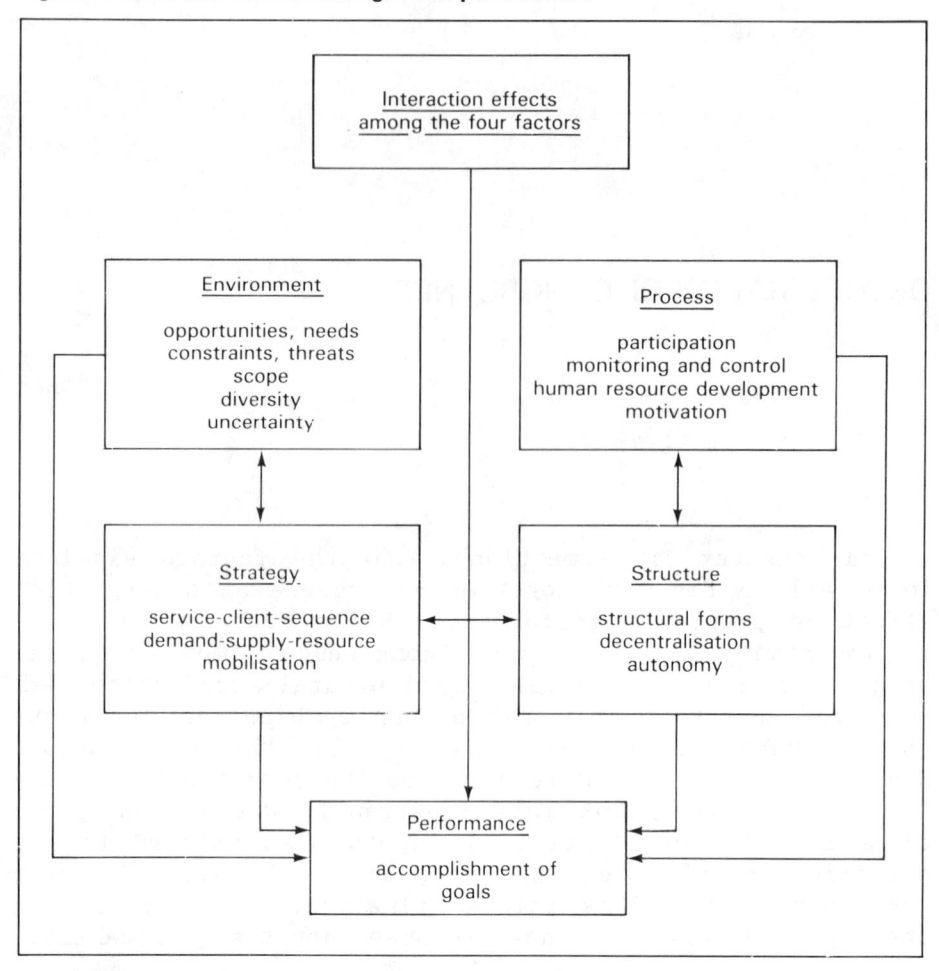

```
                    ┌─────────────────────────┐
                    │   Interaction effects   │
                    │   among the four factors│
                    └─────────────────────────┘
                                 │
          ┌──────────────────────┴──────────────────────┐
          ▼                                             ▼
┌──────────────────────┐                    ┌──────────────────────┐
│     Environment      │                    │       Process        │
│ opportunities, needs │                    │    participation     │
│  constraints, threats│                    │ monitoring and control│
│        scope         │                    │human resource development│
│      diversity       │                    │      motivation      │
│     uncertainty      │                    │                      │
└──────────┬───────────┘                    └──────────┬───────────┘
           ▲                                           ▲
           ▼                                           ▼
┌──────────────────────┐                    ┌──────────────────────┐
│      Strategy        │                    │      Structure       │
│service-client-sequence│◄──────────────────►│  structural forms   │
│demand-supply-resource│                    │  decentralisation    │
│     mobilisation     │                    │      autonomy        │
└──────────┬───────────┘                    └──────────┬───────────┘
           │                                           │
           └──────────────┐         ┌──────────────────┘
                          ▼         ▼
                    ┌─────────────────────┐
                    │    Performance      │
                    │  accomplishment of  │
                    │        goals        │
                    └─────────────────────┘
```

8.1 The meaning of congruence

Policy makers and programme managers often lose sight of the "synergy" phenomenon. Policy makers usually emphasise only one relevant factor at a time. For example, programme design often receives much attention at one time while decentralisation of structures or monitoring may receive exclusive attention at another. Each of these may surface as a serious problem on different occasions. What is ignored, however, is that these must be viewed together with all other factors shown in figure 11. The strength of strategic management lies in its ability to help us see their totality and to stimulate the search for congruent combinations.

Let us illustrate a congruent combination. Consider a national environment with diverse types of beneficiaries scattered throughout a large country. What should be the strategy of an agricultural development programme to be launched there? Should it attempt to promote many diverse crops simultaneously? Where the environment is diverse, the strategy should first promote a single crop or a few related crops and expand in phases. The input services for the same crop in different parts of the country may have to be organised differently, testing them first in the field. The diverse requirements of different groups of farmers often calls for a decentralised structure. The programme may have to elicit the response of farmers through an imaginative use of economic incentives (e.g. remunerative prices). One specific combination of strategic, structural and process interventions may turn out to be more appropriate than any other. It would be too difficult to operate this large programme with diverse beneficiaries with a centralised structure. A motivation process that ignores economic incentives would elicit little response from the beneficiaries. Viewed thus, congruence among factors crucially influences programme performance. If the combination lacks congruence, excellence in one factor cannot possibly compensate for the weakness in others. An innovative programme not supported by an adequate structure will fail. A well-designed structure lacking proper internal processes will fail too. A decentralised structure with weak monitoring processes poorly managed, or with untrained or poorly motivated field staff will also fail. The secret of strategic management lies in the "orchestration of congruence".

8.2 Congruent combinations: some illustrations

We have discussed many strategic, structural and process interventions. Their proper combination can be worked out only when one understands the programme goals as well as its environment. In order to show how congruent combinations vary under different conditons, in figure 12 we present a simplified, yet suggestive diagram which shows a few, selected interventions. This illustrates the concept of congruence without claiming to be comprehensive. The reader may wish to add other dimensions of strategy, structure and processes and see whether a more complete and congruent set of interventions could be identified for each of the quadrants of the diagram.

Figure 12 Congruent combinations

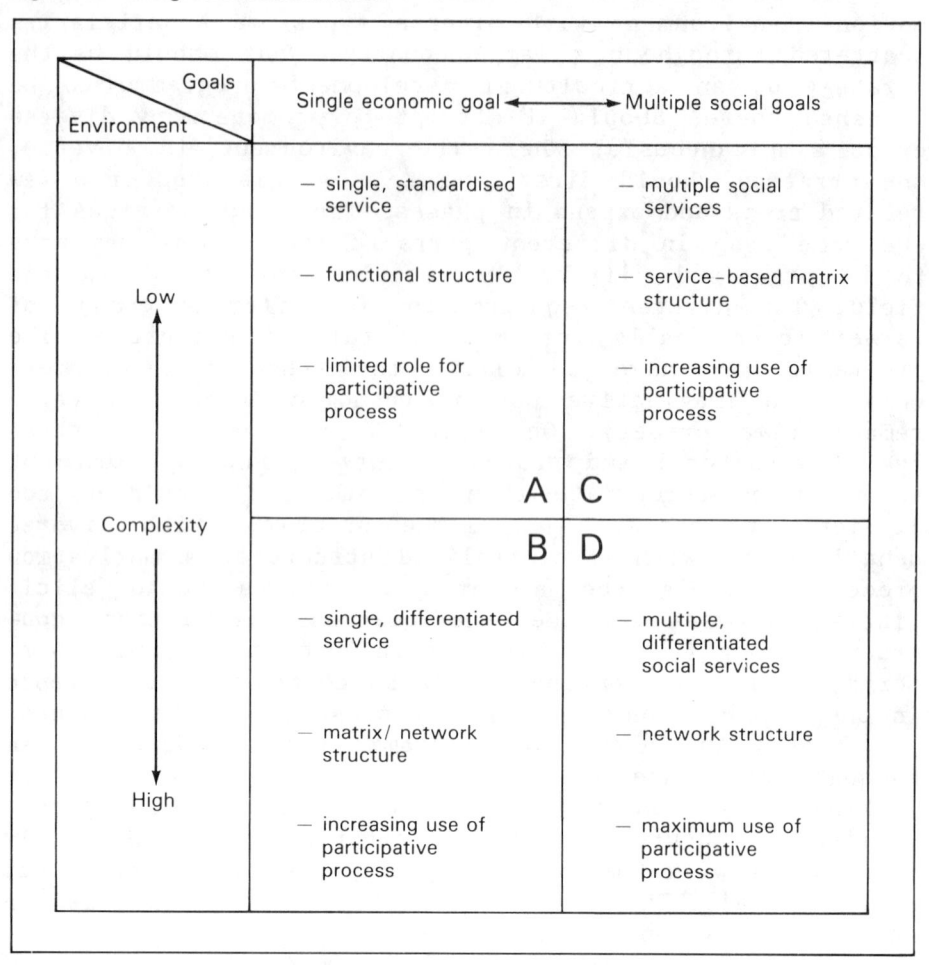

Environment \ Goals	Single economic goal ←——→ Multiple social goals	
Low ↑ Complexity	— single, standardised service — functional structure — limited role for participative process	— multiple social services — service-based matrix structure — increasing use of participative process
	A | C	
	B | D	
↓ High	— single, differentiated service — matrix/ network structure — increasing use of participative process	— multiple, differentiated social services — network structure — maximum use of participative process

Programme types

First, our diagram divides programmes into four categories. Programmes are classified according to "goals" as well as their "environmental complexity". Goals may be primarily economic or social. Programmes with mixed goals are not shown here. Some programmes have a single goal, others have multiple goals. The diagram, for the sake of simplicity, divides programmes into two extremes in a wide spectrum of goals. Complexity increases as one moves from a single economic goal to multiple social goals.

Irrespective of goals, the environmental complexity

varies. Increased diversity, uncertainty and scope add to environmental complexity, as discussed in chapter 4. Though many shades of complexity exist, we have illustrated in the diagrams only two, "high" and "low" complexity. The two dimensions of environmental complexity and goal complexity give us four categories which we shall call types A, B, C and D. Type A programmes have simple environments and a single economic goal. Type B programmes also have a single economic goal, but are environmentally complex. Type C programmes are environmentally simple with multiple goals. Type D programmes have multiple social goals and high environmental complexity.

Though these seem abstract, it is easy to find real life examples. Thus, many small single-purpose economic programmes operating in limited and homogeneous regions come close to type A (road development, electrification, etc.). National programmes focusing on specific commodities and operating in diverse, unstable environments correspond to type B (programmes for wheat, cash crops, small industry, etc.). Local or regional integrated development programmes offering multiple social services resemble type C (small urban or rural development programmes). Extremely large national programmes for integrated rural development operating under diverse conditions fall under type D. Therefore, we can relate the congruent combinations shown against the four types of programmes we see around us.

Figure 12 shows only three interventions in each programme type though many others might be considered[1]. These three interventions illustrate how congruence leads to good strategic programme management. The logic applied to their congruence can be extended to other interventions as well.

Some illustrations

Assume that type A is an agricultural development programme. A single economic goal implies a sharp focus as in programmes for single commodities, such as rice, wheat,

---

[1] See chapters 5, 6 and 7 for a comprehensive set of strategic, structural and process interventions. Strategic, structural and process interventions are represented in the set shown in figure 12.

etc. Environmental complexity (diversity, uncertainty and scope) is low. This would occur where there is little diversity among farmers, fairly stable conditions in cropping and the programme covers only a small region. Low environmental complexity allows management to adopt a single standardised service to integrate the required inputs for the farmers. Service can be standardised where beneficiaries face similar problems. If, instead of a crop, the programme focuses on a single task such as extension or credit, the same logic applies. Extension services, too, can be standardised when farmers face similar problems. This strategic intervention fits the programme goals and environmental conditions.

A functional structure fits a single, standardised service. The basic functions supporting the service are the main consideration in structuring a programme agency. Multiple services usually require other structures.

The limited role of the participative process reflects both the strategy and structure. A standardised single service and low environmental complexity imply that planning and implementation can be centralised. Beneficiaries usually respond to economic incentives even if their participation in the programme's decision making is limited. In other words, while participation is valuable in itself, the economic programme will probably succeed even if participation is limited. The process intervention indicated against type A is therefore consistent with the other two interventions discussed above.

Any departure from these three interventions could be shown to be too costly or inefficient for the programme. Thus matrix structures, which are often difficult to manage, are rarely needed by programmes offering a single service. Multiple services designed for different groups of farmers are unnecessary when diversity among them is low. The congruent combination indicated for type A, therefore, is _optimal_ (efficient) from the standpoint of performance.

The combination of interventions for type B is distinctly different from type A. While the programme goal remains the same, type B's environmental complexity is higher. The strategic intervention is a single, but differentiated service. This can be interpreted as follows:

beneficiaries are more diverse in type B. Services must be adapted to varying local conditions. The service is thus differen- tiated according to the needs and problems of different groups of beneficiaries. A standardised service would simply fail to meet the requirements of all but a few beneficiaries.

The need for local adaptation and the increased scope of the programme (e.g. national scope) call for a more decentralised structure because many decisions will have to be made in the field. The organisational structure therefore approximates a matrix or network form. Joint decision making, problem solving and action rather than the use of hierarchical control become necessary to implement the strategy. In turn, this implies the participation of beneficiaries in decision making and action, and the recruitment of staff willing to take initiatives.

Again, this set of strategic, structural and process interventions is congruent. The structural and process interventions shown against type A would have been too weak for type B, given its environment and the need to offer differentiated services. For example, increased decentralisation and reduced participation would be incongruent and hence inefficient for achieving the programme goals.

Types C and D have multiple social goals. A comparison between the two shows how, as environmental complexity increases, the need to differentiate multiple social services and to adopt a decentralised network structure becomes imperative. These interventions in turn must be reinforced by strong participative processes. This is illustrated in large integrated rural development programmes. The larger the geographical coverage, the more necessary it is to adapt these services to diverse local conditions. Planning and delivery necessitate collaboration among several organisations, possibly both public and private, with no single agency fully controlling the entire range of tasks. Only if decisions and actions are taken participatively, can the programme goals be achieved. The interventions required by type D are distinctly different from those in type A. Each set must be congruent with its envi- ronment and goals.

We cannot, therefore, prescribe a standard set of

management interventions for all types of programmes. The trick lies in finding a combination that matches the programme objectives and environment. The fit creates congruence.

As the environment or programme goals change, new interventions are needed. The questions about congruence must be asked again. In other words, congruent combinations do not last forever. When conditions change, the search for congruence must start afresh.

In this chapter we have discussed the most critical aspect of strategic management; the orchestration of congruence. In preceding chapters, we offered several guidelines on strategic management. Unfortunately, no simple guidelines can yet be offered for orchestrating congruence. Putting the components together is facilitated by an understanding of the programme environment and the nature of the objectives. Questions which help create congruence include:

1. How well do the strategic, structural and process interventions fit the environment of the programme?

2. Is there any evidence of inconsistency among the different interventions?

3. Are there any major changes in the programme environment that necessitate a redesign of any of the interventions?

4. Is the programme or government leadership committed and stable enough to facilitate the orchestration of congruence?

PUTTING STRATEGIC MANAGEMENT INTO ACTION

9

How does a programme manager put strategic management into action? Both policy makers and programme managers are bound to ask this question if they are convinced about the practical value of strategic management. The way this approach will be introduced depends on each programme's unique setting. Thus, a standardised manual is neither feasible nor likely to be of much value. It is useful, however, to highlight some important areas of early action that practitioners should bear in mind when they plan to introduce strategic management.

These are presented below in two sections. Section 9.1 suggests ideas and experiences of interest mainly to those in charge of designing and organising new programmes. Section 9.2 focuses on existing programmes that can still be improved if their management and co-ordination is re-examined in the light of what has been discussed in this book. These guidelines are not to be confused with a step-by-step sequence of what managers should do. Rather, they should be treated as the critical actions and moves to be initiated by policy makers and managers in order to make strategic management work.

9.1 Preparing new development programmes

Strategic thinking precedes project formulation

Strategic management should begin when a programme idea is born. It may be too late to think about it when a programme is already under way. However, this error is common in development planning. Programme formulation should be seen as a key part of the strategic management process. Programmes which are uncritically imported or formulated as mere techno-economic packages will probably be redesigned considerably if only the questions raised in the preceding chapters are asked and answered in time. These design changes are likely to be critical to programme success.

The initial ideas for new development programmes usually originate in ministries or government departments. Sometimes inter-ministerial task forces and donor agencies initiate project and programme ideas. The key actors in these agencies, who play an entrepreneurial role, can take several steps to facilitate strategic management. They must set the broad objectives for the programme; identify a suitable leader to be in charge of the new programme at an early stage, and encourage him to think in terms of strategic management from the outset. They must jointly agree with the programme leader on the operating goals, grant adequate autonomy, and monitor performance as the programme gets off the ground. Thus the ministry or department that launches the development programme could create essential pre-conditions for the practice of strategic management.

Clear understanding of government objectives

Before the programme manager arrives on the scene, the government will have formulated the broad objectives for the programme. He should, therefore, start by understanding and seeking clarifications on these objectives. Policy makers can facilitate this by discussing objectives and their implications with programme managers at an early stage. The broader the objectives, the greater the programme leaders room for manoeuvre. He will be best able to choose operating goals consistent with his environment early when his flexibility is the greatest. If, on the other hand, the government has defined programme objectives narrowly and in operational terms, the programme manager will have a more difficult task. He must then evolve his strategy taking into account the limitations imposed by government. In either case, the programme manager must make every effort to understand and interpret the given objectives before he starts designing his strategy.

Analysing the environment and influencing key actors

Designing programmes without considering the unique features of their environments is a common error. Technocrats, administrators and donor agencies are often enamoured of certain technologies and carried away by their conviction as to what the people should do. This is most harmful in social development programmes, e.g. in rural development, adult education, nutrition, etc. A programme manager could avoid this pitfall by taking time to understand the forces operating in his environment including the motivations of the key actors and groups (e.g. beneficiaries, local leaders, etc.) likely to be affected by his programme. Strategy formulation should not be viewed as a purely technical exercise or as a task to be left to a set of specialists who are not sensitive to what goes on in the programme's environment. Of the different elements described in chapter 4, the motivations of the beneficiaries and the staff, and the constraints imposed by the governmental structures and decision making processes, should be considered very early. Equally important is the careful assessment of the actors who may have either positive or negative impacts on the programme. The strategy must suggest how to influence these actors to support the programme. The programme manager should use both formal and informal ways of probing the environment and cultivate this skill in his team members.

While staff support can aid environmental analysis, the top management of a development programme should be continually sensitive to the environment and regard its interpretation as a key task. For example, sensitive political changes or shifts in political or bureaucratic coalitions in the national environment may have implications for a given programme. It is the programme leader who is more likely to sense such changes and their potential impact on his tasks. Younger staff members may or may not always be sensitive to such environmental changes or adept at proposing strategic responses to these emerging developments. Strategic management should not be viewed as the work of a specialised unit. It properly belongs to programme leaders.

Pilot projects

When formal and comprehensive analysis of the environment is not feasible, a pilot project is usually the best way to acquire environmental insights. Here, the emphasis should be on initiating pilot projects at the very outset and building their lessons into the programme for replication. Where this is not possible, pilot experiments should be undertaken after the programme starts. The understanding and insights generated by them can still be fed into the ongoing programme. Pilot project experience often already exists, in which case the manager should learn from it. Failure to integrate the learning from pilot projects has been a major problem in many countries. Programme managers should certainly try to recruit persons who have played key roles in successful pilot projects, as this is one of the most effective ways of learning from these experiments.

However, one pitfall is to be avoided: do not assume that the programme can be managed in the same style as the pilot project. The pilot project may have benefited from particularly favourable material and staffing conditions or paid special attention to project monitoring to make it successful. Learning from pilot projects also includes reviewing such special conditions. The question is: will it be possible to create the same or similar conditions for the whole programme? What needs to be done to create such conditions? If not, what adaptations or innovative responses are needed?

Phased replication

A frequent error is to expand a programme without realistically assessing the problems of managing fast expansion. A phased plan for expansion facilitates strategic management because programme managers then have an opportunity to learn and absorb as they move along. Simultaneous expansion all over the country can hurt this learning process a great deal. Political leaders are seldom sensitive to the risks of fast expansion. It is the duty of programme managers to make them aware of such risks and to persuade them to avoid the "grand slam" approach.

Autonomy appropriate to the programme's tasks

Once the objectives are known and the complexity of the environment appreciated, a programme manager should assess the degree of organisational autonomy his programme agency requires. Admittedly, this is easier to do in new programmes. In ongoing programmes, the pattern is set and change is more difficult. But even in new programmes, managers are often reluctant to raise the question of "autonomy". This may be a serious mistake. When a programme is being evolved, a programme manager can often influence his ministry's thinking on autonomy by demonstrating how limited autonomy can reduce the programme's performance and success. Certainly, the early planning phase is the right time to seek autonomy. If the manager fails to get the autonomy he sought, he may have to work towards earning it, as explained in chapter 6. The point to remember is that the question of autonomy should be raised well before the programme design and structure are frozen, not afterwards.

9.2 Applying strategic management to ongoing programmes

Clearly, applying strategic management is an uphill task for a manager who takes over an ongoing programme. He has inherited strategies and structures. Work habits and practices are difficult to modify overnight. Needless to say, if an ongoing programme is in serious trouble, a new manager may well be given adequate powers and autonomy to redress the situation. But even where this flexibility is not granted, programme managers can do several other things to pave the way for strategic management.

Operational versus strategic management

In theory, there should be no conflict between strategic and operational management, the latter being used to implement strategy and monitor the everyday course of a development programme. In practice, however, many senior administrators and managers are totally absorbed in the day-to-day problems of operations. They claim that they have little time for strategic management. In reality, their problem is that they spend too much time on operational problems. They usually argue that middle managers and officials at lower levels are neither competent nor motivated to make the right decisions. The answer lies in strengthening the skills and motivation of the staff through training and development. When little attention is given to equipping people to perform their tasks well, it is not surprising that they are unable to discharge their duties. This important area in programme management deserves urgent attention. Top managers will be able to devote more time to issues of strategic management only when they develop their subordinates and delegate operational decisions increasingly to them.

Strategic audit

It is often possible to initiate a formal comprehensive review of an ongoing programme to identify and evaluate strategy that has been followed since programme inception and propose changes in strategy and in the management system of the programme. Such a strategic audit might follow the line of thought presented in this book, using the questions given at the end of chapters 2 to 8. In any case, the programme goal and objectives, environment, strategic choices, resources, organisational structure and internal processes must be reviewed.

This might be time-consuming and technically difficult. Also, political objections may be raised and resistance to change found among the managers who have developed certain habits and who might think that strategic management would demand more than their competence and commitment permit.

There is, therefore, an important question of tactics: how should a strategic review of a programme be started so that it has a good chance of success right from the start? In particular, programme managers must consider the attitudes and policies of government as well as the experience and attitudes of the managerial staff. Thus, there might be situations where a strategic review of an ongoing programme should start from the outside, e.g. by appointing a review committee to examine the facts, interview all people concerned and come up with concrete proposals for changes. However, such external review committees might often be perceived by the programme managers as too administrative a tool for solving complex technical and human problems, and even good review reports may be given no follow-up. Initiating a strategic review from the inside with the active participation of the programme manager may be a more viable approach. The group should start by identifying the key problems faced by the programme and the causes of deficient performance. This tends to be more effective for three reasons: (1) the analysis can be concrete, starting from the problems faced by the staff in everyday operations; (2) it can be an important learning exercise, since analytical, planning and other skills of managers will increase during the exercise, and (3) it generates more commitment to applying and utilising new ideas and proposals thus developed than would be the case if the proposals came from an external body known to the managers concerned only through a few interviews.[1]

If inadequacies in strategic management are identified, the programme manager should initiate action to inform, educate and influence the key actors in his supervising ministry and other collaborating agencies (if he has to manage a network structure). This has to be done tactfully, in both formal and informal ways. Obviously, the ability to build relationships and demonstrate how common (shared) goals could be achieved through the proposed changes will come in handy at this stage. This applies particularly where a programme manager has to achieve his goals through collaboration with a network of agencies. A great deal will depend on how much bargaining power or clout he has vis-à-vis his ministry and other agencies.

Step-by-step approach to changes

Where reforms are necessary and feasible, the wise manager does not start with the most difficult and complex changes. Resistance and organisational problems will be more severe here. Instead he should attempt to introduce simpler performance inducing changes. For example, initiating a participative planning process with the staff or introducing a simple, yet regular monitoring system may help to build confidence and credibility, and in the process prepare the ground for more complex changes necessary for strategic management. This means that while the programme manager needs an over-all concept of the directions in which the programme should move, he is prepared to feel his way through, for tactical reasons. This ap-

---

[1] Of interest in this connection is an ILO publication describing a problem identification and problem solving approach used in a number of public agencies. See R. Abramson and W. Halset: Planning for improved enterprise performance: A guide for managers and consultants (Geneva, International Labour Office, 1979).

proach may take considerable time in the case of complex ongoing programmes. But this approach is likely to be more rewarding than attempts to rush in with a formidable set of drastic reforms. In the final analysis, it is the programme manager in consultation with his ministry who should decide on the alternative most appropriate in his situation.

Workshops and seminars

Many managers of development programmes have never had an opportunity to exchange experiences about strategic management with their peers and learn about new trends in the practice and theory of strategic management in training workshops and seminars. In general, more such training is needed in most developing countries. However, general lectures and discussions, based on foreign materials and experience, are not enough. Wherever possible, strategic management workshops should be tailor-made and pay considerable attention to the specific problems that exist in given programmes. Theoretical knowledge can also be provided, but this has to be related to concrete problems faced by the managers involved. The managers' active participation is to be encouraged; it may well be that such a workshop will become an effective starting point for an internal strategic review of an important development programme.

Using consultants

Training efforts can be coupled with consultancy on strategic management. Sometimes, consultancy may be the best starting point, especially if the top management is convinced of the need to introduce strategic management. Often, a combination of consultancy and training turns out to be a powerful tool. Consultancy should not be viewed as a mere "design job" with the consultants disappearing as soon as the report is finished. Consultants should see through the critical phase of implementation and assist in resolving issues and providing training support wherever necessary. While this approach is well known in industry, in development programmes consultancy is often viewed as a one-shot affair. Hence the need to emphasise the continuing and supportive nature of the role consultants ought to play in the development context. Management schools and consulting organisations must both recognise this requirement and assist programme leaders in appreciating the importance of this approach.

However, not all consultants fully appreciate the special problems of managing development programmes, and there is an urgent need to train more consultants who do. Thus, programme managers who decide to invite consultancy organisations to help implement strategic management should carefully specify their requests and screen the proposals to ensure that the consultants are fully competent, both in strategic management and the problems of development programmes.

9.3 Taking action

This book has been designed to help programme managers think about and practise strategic management. They should view training, consultancy, internal re- views and audit exercises as useful steps that lead to action. It is important, therefore, that they are clear in their own minds as to how interventions should be planned and sequenced to achieve this goal. A programme leader who is ready to initiate the process of strategic management should ensure that his team of managers are active, committed participants in this endeavour. Where the initiator or change agent is not the programme leader, he must take special care to win the commitment and full participation of the programme leadership, including managers at all relevant levels. The workshops, training programmes and consultancy activities, and other joint exercises referred to in earlier sections, are experiences which the entire team should share together. The very process of sharing these experiences helps improve mutual understanding and committment to shared goals, clarifies broader constraints and provides a common language and mode of thinking which facilitates communication.

The programme leader and his top team should view the exercise as one of _learning by doing_. The guidelines and criteria in this book are unlikely to yield blueprints ready for mechanical implementation. Rather, they are more likely to lead to ideas on interventions which need to be tried out, modified and improved as experience is gained and adaptations to changing conditions are made.

Appendix 1
Further reading

Books

Abramson R. and Halset W.: Planning for improved enterprise performance: A guide for managers and consultants Management Development Series No. 15 (Geneva, International Labour Office, 1979).

Ackoff R.: Redesigning the future: A systems approach to societal problems (New York, Wiley, 1974).

Andrews K.: The concept of corporate strategy (Homewood, Illinois, Irwin, 1980).

Ansoff H.I.: Implanting strategic management (Englewood Cliffs, New Jersey, Prentice-Hall, 1984).

Austin J.: Strategic management in developing countries (In press, 1989).

Bardach E.: The implementation game: What happens after a bill becomes a law (Cambridge, Massachusetts, MIT Press, 1977).

Beer M., Spector B., Lawrence P.R., Mills D.Q. and Walton R.E.: Managing human assets (New York, Free Press, 1984).

Benor D. and Harrison J.Q.: Agricultural extension: The training and visit system (Washington, DC, The World Bank, 1977).

Bryant C. and White L.: Managing development in the Third World (Boulder, Colorado, Westview Press, 1982).

Bryson J.: Strategic planning for public and non-profit organizations: A link to sustaining organization achievement (Jessey-Bros. Inc., 1989).

Caiden N. and Wildavsky A.: Planning and budgeting in poor countries (New York, Wiley, 1974).

Carner G. and Korten D.C.: People-centered planning: The USAID/Philippines experience, NASPAA Working Paper No. 2 (Washington, DC, National Association of Schools of Public Affairs and Administration, 1982).

Chambers R.: Managing rural development: Ideas and experience from East Africa (Uppsala, Scandinavian Institute of African Studies, 1974).

Chambers R.: Rural poverty unperceived: Problems and remedies, World Bank Staff Working Paper No. 400 (Washington, DC, The World Bank, 1980).

Churchman C.W.: The design of inquiring systems: Basic concepts of systems and organisation (New York, Basic Books, 1971).

Cohen J.: Integrating services for rural development (Cambridge, Massachusetts, Lincoln Institute of Land Policy and Kennedy School of Government, 1979).

Cohen J.M. and Uphoff N.T.: Rural development participation: Concepts and measures for project design, implementation and evaluation (Ithaca, New York, Cornell University, Rural Development Committee, 1977).

Colle R. et al: Paraprofessionals in rural development (Ithaca, New York, Cornell University, Rural Development Committee, 1979).

Friedmann J. and Weaver C.: Territory and functions: The evolution of regional planning (Berkeley, California, University of California Press, 1979).

Gable R. and Springer J.F.: Administering agricultural development in Asia: A comparative analysis of four national programmes (Boulder, Colorado, Westview Press, 1976).

Galbraith J.: *Organisation design* (Reading, Massachusetts, Addison-Wesley, 1977).

Galbraith J. and Nathason D.A.: *Strategy implementation: The role of structure and process* (St. Paul, Minnesota, West Publishing Co., 1978).

Gant G.: *Development administration: Concepts, goals, methods* (Madison, University of Wisconsin Press, 1979).

Gilbert N. and Specht H.: *Co-ordinating social services: An analysis of community, organisational and staff characteristics* (New York, Praeger, 1977).

Giridhar G., et. al.: *Readings in population programme management* (Kuala Lumpur, ICOMP, 1988).

Grindle M.S. (ed.): *Politics and policy implementation in the Third World* (Princeton, New Jersey, Princeton University Press, 1980).

Hage J. and Fristerbursch K.: *Organizational change as a development strategy: Methods and tactics for managing Third World organizations* (Boulder, Colorado, Lynne Reiner Inc., 1987).

Hargrove E.: *The missing link: The study of the implementation of social policy* (Washington, DC, The Urban Institute, 1975).

Hax A.C. (ed.): *Planning strategies that work* (New York and Oxford, Oxford University Press, 1987).

Hax A.C. and Majluf N.S.: *Strategic management: An integrative perspective* (Englewood Cliffs, New Jersey, Prentice-Hall, 1984).

Hellriegel D. and Slocum J.W.: *Management: A contingency approach* (Reading, Massachusetts, Addison-Wesley, 1974).

Hirschman A.: *Development projects observed* (Washington, DC, The Brookings Institution, 1967).

Honadle G. and Klauss R. (eds): *International development administration: Implementation analysis for development projects* (New York, Praeger, 1979).

Hunter G.: *The administration of agricultural development: Lessons from India* (London, Oxford University Press, 1970).

Hyden G.: *Efficiency versus distribution in East African co-operatives: A study in organisational conflict* (Nairobi, East African Literature Bureau, 1973).

Ickis J.: *Strategy and structure in rural development*, Doctoral dissertation (Boston, Massachusetts, Harvard Business School, 1978).

Ickis J., et. al.: *Beyond bureaucracy: The strategic management of social development* (West Hartford, Connecticut, Kumarian Press, 1986).

Iglesias G. (ed.): *Implementation: The problem of achieving results* (Manila, Eastern Regional Organisation for Public Administration, 1976).

Ingle M.D.: *Implementing development programmes: A state-of-the-art review* (Washington, DC, United States Agency for International Development, 1979).

Israel A.: *Institutional development* (Baltimore, Maryland, Johns Hopkins Press, 1987).

Jain S.C. et al. (eds): *Management development in population programmes* (North Carolina School of Public Health, 1981).

Jedlicka A.: *Organisation for rural development: Risk taking and appropriate technology* (New York, Praeger, 1977).

Khandwalla P.N.: *The design of organisations* (New York, Harcourt Brace, 1977).

Knight K. (ed.): *Matrix management: A cross-functional approach to management* (Farnborough, Hants, Gower Press, 1977).

Knight P.T. (ed.): *Implementing programmes of human development*, World Bank Staff Working Paper No. 403 (Washington, DC, The World Bank, 1980).

Korten D.C. (ed.): Population and social development management: A challenge for management schools (Caracas, IESA, 1979).

Korten D.C. and Alfonso P. (eds): Bureaucracy and the poor: Closing the gap (Singapore, McGraw-Hill, 1981).

Lawrence P. and Lorsch J.W.: Organisation and environment: Managing differentiation and integration (Homewood, Illinois, Irwin, 1969).

Lele U.: The design of rural development: lessons from Africa (Baltimore, Maryland, Johns Hopkins University Press, 1975).

Leonard D.: Reaching the peasant farmer: Organisation theory and practice in Kenya (Chicago, Illinois, University of Chicago Press, 1977).

Lorsch J. and Allen S.: Managing diversity and interdependence (Boston, Massachusetts, Harvard Business School, 1973).

MacMillan I.: Strategy formulation: Political concepts (St. Paul, Minnesota, West Publishing, 1978).

March J. and Simon H.: Organisations (New York, Wiley, 1950).

Mintzberg H.: The nature of managerial work (New York, Harper and Row, 1973).

Moris J.: Managing induced rural development (Bloomington, Indiana, International Development Institute, Indiana University, 1981).

Mosher A.: Thinking about rural development (New York, Agricultural Development Council, 1976).

Owens E. and Shaw R.: Development reconsidered: Bridging the gap between government and people (Lexington, Massachusetts, D.C. Heath and Co., 1972).

Paul S.: Managing development programmes: Lessons from success (Boulder, Colorado, Westview Press, 1982).

Pyle D.F.: *From project to programme: Structural constraints associated with expansion*, NASPAA Working Paper No. 3 (Washington, DC, National Association of Schools of Public Affairs and Administration, 1982).

Pressman J. and Wildavsky A.: *Implementation* (Berkeley, California, University of California Press, 1973).

Riggs F.: *Administration in developing countries* (Boston, Massachusetts, Houghton Mifflin Co., 1964).

Rumelt R.: *Strategy, structure and economic performance* (Boston, Massachusetts, Harvard Business School, 1974).

Siffin W.: *Administrative problems and integrated rural development* (Bloomington, Indiana, International Development Institute, Indiana University, 1979).

Smith W., Letham F.J. and Thoolen B.A.: *The design of organisations for rural development projects - A progress report*, World Bank Staff Working Paper No. 375 (Washington, DC, The World Bank, 1980).

Stout R.: *Management or control? The organisational challenge* (Bloomington, Indiana, Indiana University Press, 1980).

World Bank: *Rural development: Sector policy paper* (Washington, DC, 1975).

Articles

Ahmad Y.: "Administration of integrated rural development programme: A note on methodology", in *International Labour Review*, Feb. 1975, pp. 119-142.

Armor T., Honadle G., Olson C. and Weisel P.: "Organising and supporting integrated rural development projects: A two-fold approach to administrative development", in *Journal of Administration Overseas*, Vol. XVIII, No. 4, 1979, pp. 276-286.

Arturo Israel: "Towards better project implementation", in *Finance and Development*, Mar. 1978, pp. 27-30.

Arua E.: "Improving rural development administration in Nigeria", in Agricultural Administration, Vol. 5, No. 4, 1978, pp. 285-286.

Bottrall A.: "Technology of management in irrigated agriculture", in Overseas Development Institute Review, No. 2, 1978, pp. 22-50.

Brinkerhoff D.: "Inside public bureaucracy: Empowering managers to empower clients", in Rural Development Participation Review, Vol. 1, No. 1, 1979, pp. 7-9.

Chambers R.: "Executive capacity as a scarce resource", in International Development Review, Vol. II, No. 2, June 1969.

Chase G.: "Implementing a human services programme: How hard will it be?", in Public Policy, Vol. 27, No. 4, 1979, pp. 385-423.

Esman M.: "Development administration and constituency organisation", in Development Administration, March-April 1978.

Fischer J. and Shaner W.W.: "Problems in planning integrated rural development", in Integrated Rural Development Review, Vol. 1, No. 1, 1975, pp. 36-43.

Gasson R.: "Farmers' participation in co-operative activities", in Sociologia Ruralis, Vol. 27, No. 1/2, 1977, pp. 102-123.

Khandwalla P.: "Mass output orientation of operations technology and organisation structure", in Administrative Science Quarterly, No. 19, 1974, pp. 74-97.

Korten D.C.: "Community organisation and rural development: A learning process approach", in Public Administration Review, Vol. 58, Autumn 1980.

Miles R. and Snow C.: "Organizations: New concepts for new focus", in California Management Review, Spring, 1986.

Montgomery J.: "Allocation of authority in land reform programmes: A comparative study of administrative process and outputs", in Administrative Science Quarterly, Vol. 17, No. 1, 1972, pp. 62-75.

Montgomery J.: "The populist front in rural development: Or shall we eliminate the bureaucrats and get on with the job?", in Public Administration Review, Vol. 39, No. 1, 1979.

Morris J.: "Administrative authority and the problem of effective agricultural administration in East Africa", in African Review, Vol. 2, No. 1, June, 1972.

Negandhi A. and Raimann B.: "A contingency theory on organisation re-examined in the context of a developing country", in Academy of Management Journal, No. 15, 1972, pp. 137-146.

Paul S.: "The strategic management of development programmes: Evidence from an international study", in The International Review of Administrative Sciences, No. 1, 1983.

Paul S.: "Lessons of India's Goitre Control Programme", in World Health Forum, Vol. 7, 1986.

Paul S. and Subramonian A.: "Development programmes for the poor: Do strategies make a difference?", in Economic and Political Weekly, 5 March 1983.

Pennings J.: "The relevance of the structural contingency model for organisational effectiveness", in Administrative Science Quarterly, No. 20, 1975, pp. 393-410.

Rondinelli D.: "National investment planning and equity policy in developing countries: The challenge of decentralised administration", in Policy Sciences, Vol. 10, 1975, pp. 105-118.

Rondinelli D. and Jones B.A.: "Decision-making, managerial capacity and development: An entrepreneurial approach to planning", in African Administrative Studies, Vol. 13, 1975, pp. 105-118.

Ruttan V.: "Integrated rural development programmes: A sceptical perspective", in International Development Review, No. 4, 1975.

Schein E.H.: "Coming to a new awareness of organizational culture", in Sloan Management Review, Winter 1984, pp.3-16.

Steers R.: "Antecedents and outcomes of organisational commitment", in Administrative Science Quarterly, Vol. 22, No. 1, 1977, pp.46-56.

Tichy N.M. and Ulrich D.O.: "The leadership challenge: A call for the transformational leader", in Sloan Management Review, Fall 1984, pp. 59-68.

Tichy N.M., Fombrun C.J. and Devanna M.A.: "Strategic human resource management", in Sloan Management Review, Winter 1982, pp. 47-61.

Wade R.: "Leadership and integrated rural development: reflections on an Indian success story", in Journal of Administration Overseas, Vol. 17, No. 4, 1978.

Zaman M.A.: "Some experiences in the implementation of integrated rural development (IRD) programmes", in Agricultural Administration, Vol. 4, 1977, pp. 306-307.

Appendix 2
Glossary of selected strategic management terms

<u>Autonomy</u>: the degree of freedom a programme agency enjoys from its parent ministry/department in important areas of decision making and action, such as internal fund allocation, operational plans for service delivery, recruitment, remuneration and promotion of personnel.

<u>Demand mobilisation</u>: the use of media, incentives, participation and leadership to make beneficiaries and the general public aware of and utilise a programme. This implies the use of financial, physical and human resources to provide services to meet mobilised demand.

<u>Dominant goal</u>: a clear, well focused, major objective of a programme expressed in qualitative and quantitative terms.

<u>Economic incentives</u>: include the economic benefits and bonuses available to staff members and the prices paid to suppliers.

<u>Effective autonomy</u>: the degree of autonomy an organisation actually enjoys, which may differ from that defined in its legal charter.

<u>Environment</u>: those forces outside a programme which create opportunities for, as well as constraints on, its growth. Forces inside an organisation's boundaries are generally subject to management <u>control</u>. Important forces outside its boundaries, in its environment, can only be influenced, or if not <u>influenced</u>, must be understood and appreciated.

Functional structure: where an organisation's tasks are divided according to its functions and these tasks are integrated hierarchically and performed according to rules and authority.

Information systems: the procedures for reporting, monitoring and for reviewing and controlling the achievement of objectives.

Matrix structure: a form of organisation designed to focus on both diverse outputs or services and the functions relevant to them. Under this arrangement, many members of staff simultaneously report to two bosses. Thus there is a dual authority (control) structure.

Network structure: where several public or private agencies must formally collaborate to achieve common goals, but where the lead agency cannot exercise direct hierarchical control over participating agencies. Sources of influence used to achieve collaboration include joint planning and review of activities, control over budget (resource allocation) and common membership of committees.

Nominal autonomy: the legally defined extent to which an organisation can depart from the norms and practices of its parent organisation.

Organisation structure: the durable arrangements within a programme agency by which it performs its tasks. These include the distribution of authority and responsibility, the reporting relationships and the co-ordinating machinery.

Organisational processes: the instruments for influencing the behaviour of staff and beneficiaries of a programme. These include the goal setting and resource allocation (budgeting) methods, the monitoring, evaluation and control processes, the human resource development (selection and training) systems of a programme and the motivational processes (use of incentives, creation of commitment).

Personnel selection and development: the process of attracting the best available people, hiring them and training them to do their jobs as well as possible.

Pilot project: a small project undertaken to test and adapt a development approach to a particular social and geographic situation.

Sequential diversification: a strategy under which the programme starts with a single service and subsequently moves into other services. This reduces managerial complexity and is a good strategy, especially when services are diverse, unrelated and difficult to measure.

Sources of influence: the groups of people or organisations that programme managers can count on in getting laws changed or funds allocated.

Strategic management: the inter-related top management interventions which provide the framework for operational decisions and actions to accomplish programme goals.

Strategy: the set of long-term choices the programme leaders make in terms of goals, services, policies and action plans.

Structural differentiation: dividing organisational tasks/functions into manageable components.

Structural integration: putting together the differentiated organisational tasks or components to achieve the over-all objectives of the programme or agency.

Technological change: the process of improving the way activities are performed and the way tools, methods and equipment are employed.